BOREDOM AND THE RELIGIOUS

IMAGINATION

STUDIES IN RELIGION AND CULTURE

Frank Burch Brown, Gary L. Ebersole,
and Edith Wyschogrod, *Editors*

BOREDOM
AND THE
RELIGIOUS
IMAGINATION

MICHAEL L. RAPOSA

UNIVERSITY PRESS OF VIRGINIA
CHARLOTTESVILLE AND LONDON

Library of Congress Cataloging-in-Publication Data

Raposa, Michael L.
    Boredom and the religious imagination / Michael L. Raposa
    p.   cm. — (Studies in religion and culture)
    Includes bibliographical references and index.
    ISBN 0-8139-1898-7 (alk. paper). — ISBN 0-8139-1925-8
(pbk. : alk. paper)
    1. Boredom—Religious aspects. I. Title. II. Series: Studies
in religion and culture (Charlottesville, Va.)
BL625.92.R36 1999   99-28051
291.4'2—dc21   CIP

For my parents,

Louis and Laura Raposa

CONTENTS

Preface   ix

Introduction   1

1 Portraying Acedia   11

2 Killing Time: Strategies of Diversion   41

3 Nothing Matters: The Logic of Indifference   72

4 Ritual, Redundancy, and the Religious
  Imagination   105

5 Boredom, Semiosis, and Spiritual Exercises   136

Postlude: On Waiting   167

Notes   175

Index   197

PREFACE

THESE philosophical meditations on boredom trace their origins back nearly twenty years to a classroom in Connecticut. I was teaching a seminar on the religious significance of play, reading and discussing books by Huizinga, Caillois, Moltmann, Hugo Rahner, and others. Our seminar conversation was fairly uneventful and uninspiring until a particular afternoon several weeks into the course. It was at that point that one of my students suggested that we ought to focus our attention on the problem of boredom in order better to understand the nature of play, since boredom is the great enemy of play. It is boredom, more than any other single factor, that is most capable of defeating play, spoiling it, bringing it to a halt. Much to my surprise, the other students in the class, after an initial hesitation, were quite willing to talk about boredom in a serious fashion. This was a phenomenon with which they all seemed familiar; moreover, and somewhat ironically, it was a topic that they all seemed to find rather *interesting*. Our conversation flourished and the seminar was revived. I took notes.

Not long after that experience, I gave a lecture at the University of Virginia on the religious significance of boredom. A later draft of that lecture was published as an article in 1985. Responses both to the lecture and to the article confirmed what I had already learned in the classroom. Whatever the extent to which people disagreed (with me or among themselves) about the nature of boredom, its principal causes and effects, they were easily drawn into discussion of these issues (conversations that often began with tongue in cheek but typically became lively and thoughtful). This outcome proved to be somewhat novel, even surprising, for most people. While boredom is an experience that few had been able completely to circumvent, reflection on that experience had always seemed quite avoidable as a trivial pursuit. What was there to be learned from thinking about boredom? How could boredom, which signifies a lack of interest, itself prove to be interesting? A classroom discussion, a lecture, or a scholarly journal seemed to provide the framework and license for serious consideration of a topic that, otherwise, they would not have been inclined to pursue.

Whether or not this book is demonstrative of the fact, I am convinced that there is a great deal to be learned from the experience of boredom (much of it religiously edifying) and that thinking about that experience can be interesting, even enjoyable (at least for some persons, in certain circumstances). What most intrigued my students about the topic was the ambiguity of boredom, its surprisingly complex nature. My being bored with someone or something can represent a trivial matter or a matter of great consequence. My disinterest can signify either a moral failure or the presence of virtue. Boredom undermines play, and yet a certain spirit of disinterestedness is essential to playfulness. I can be bored, at least for a time, with something that I continue to care deeply about; even love cannot banish boredom altogether.

This ambiguity is typically cloaked by the mundane quality of the experience, its appearance as something ordinary, everyday, unremarkable. Indeed, if boredom conveys insight it does so quietly, without fireworks, gongs, or cymbals. To appreciate the value of boredom does not require that one should welcome, much less celebrate, its occurrence. The experience of boredom, sooner or later, now and then, seems inevitable for most persons. Regarding those experiences, I would invite my readers to shake off the veil of everydayness and simply to pay attention.

I have tried to pay attention to the insights of many persons who have shared my conversation about this topic over the years. Those insights are too numerous to have been embodied adequately in my text. And those persons are too numerous for me to recollect all of them, much less acknowledge them here. But I hope that neither the limited space of this preface nor the limited power of my memory will be construed by anyone as a lack of gratitude.

I do want to thank Corey Piccinino, the college student at Sacred Heart University, whose thoughtful observation first launched this inquiry many years ago. The students in that first class and in subsequent seminars both at Sacred Heart and at Lehigh University have enriched this study with their questions and comments, helped to motivate it with their enthusiasm. Numerous colleagues have done likewise. In particular, Gordon Bearn, Richard Grigg, Dennis Marshall, Peter Ochs, Lloyd Steffen, and Peter Van Ness all kindly agreed to read drafts of this book, supplying good advice about how it might be improved. (Their advice was consistently good; my apologies along with my thanks to them if I failed to make consistently good use of it.) Gordon also supplied me with a steady stream of bibliographical material relevant to my theme. Without his assistance, I probably would have neglected to observe how Heidegger gradually became preoccupied with boredom as a "fundamental attunement," in much the same way that a younger Heidegger had thought and written about anxiety.

Early in the development of this project, both Merold Westphal and James Ross encouraged me with their confidence that boredom was a philosophical topic worth taking seriously. As the project took shape, Cathie Brettschneider of the University Press of Virginia provided similar support, as well as patient guidance. A draft of the first two chapters was written during the summer of 1996, while I was at Brown University participating in a seminar sponsored by the National Endowment for the Humanities. My colleagues in the seminar provided a wonderful stimulus to my work with their conversation; I owe a special debt of gratitude to John Reeder and Donald Swearer, codirectors of that seminar.

My wife, Mary Ellen, has been, as always, my steadiest source of encouragement, lending me an editor's eyes and ears as well as her theological insight. She has taught me more about the special virtues of *caritas* and *fortitudo* than Aquinas ever did. Moreover, I owe an extraordinary thanks to her and to my children, Daniel, Elizabeth, and Rosemary, for helping me not to take this project too seriously.

This book is dedicated, with great love and respect, to my parents, Louis and Laura Raposa. We can learn a great deal from our boredom when we are young, especially if our parents are wise enough not constantly to distract us. For their care, for the freedom to learn, for the countless precious gifts that good parents give, I owe them my deepest gratitude.

BOREDOM AND THE RELIGIOUS

IMAGINATION

INTRODUCTION

ALTHOUGH it is reasonable to suppose that wine from the Passover Seder, combined with the lateness of the hour, were factors that ought to bear explanatory weight, I still find myself musing over the images from Gethsemane supplied by the Gospel narratives: a prayerful and passionate Jesus juxtaposed with his ineluctably *drowsy* disciples. My judgment of the disciples' behavior is a bit more complicated than the one that Jesus himself seemed to articulate. Indeed, Jesus' own analysis notwithstanding, here the weakness of the flesh seems to signify, even as it is most tangibly linked to, a deeper, spiritual malady. The symptoms of this condition are delineated most clearly in Mark's Gospel, where the disciples rather consistently fail to discern the genuine significance of what is happening in their midst. Their failure in Gethsemane to perceive the fatefulness of the hour at hand is an especially powerful instance of an ongoing difficulty. But I should expose immediately the relevance of these biblical images to my present inquiry: the con-

1

sensus of opinion, at least among medieval Christian theologians, suggests that drowsiness is one among several potential byproducts or "daughters" of acedia.

Philosophers of religious experience, as well as theologians of the spiritual life, have provided elaborate phenomenological analyses of the problem of acedia, a medieval term for spiritual sluggishness, dullness in prayer, boredom with the rituals of devotion. Acedia is traditionally perceived by theologians as a sinful condition, while philosophers like William James have described the spiritual/psychological malaise that afflicts the "sick soul."[1] Yet it is important to observe that these descriptions also bear a certain resemblance to mystical accounts of the "dark night," a terrifying but necessary stage in the mystic's spiritual journey. I want to suggest, in more general terms, that the experience of boredom, of religious "low information" states, plays an ambivalent role in the spiritual life. Boredom can serve as midwife for the birth of religious knowledge; it is the pallid half-darkness that sometimes lingers just before the dawning of religious insight. Frequently, however, it is perceived as a dangerous condition, one to be eschewed, sometimes by necessity to be endured, but certainly not to be desired or cultivated.

Every situation will probably embody, on some level and for some persons, potentially meaningful information. If this is the case, then the problem of boredom becomes at bottom a *semiotic* problem, arising from a difficulty on the part of the bored person in reading the signs or interpreting the information in any given situation *as* meaningful or interesting.[2] Moreover, insofar as religious insight is rooted in lived human experience, boredom may be symptomatic of a "breakdown" in the process that yields this insight. It represents, from a certain perspective, an epistemic blindness, not simply a refusal to pay attention but, rather, an inability to perceive the religious significance of things.

Here my concern is not systematically to defend such a perspective but rather to assess its intelligibility by exploring the role of the imagination in the process of interpretation. It is important to determine the precise sense in which boredom can be regarded as a failure of imagination. At the same time, I propose that the experience of boredom can sometimes be regarded as an essential precondition for the imagination's proper exercise. Throughout, my inquiry is guided by basic Peircean insights concerning the nature of experience as semiosis: all experience is interpreted experience and all such interpretations take the form of implicit or explicit inferences.[3] Furthermore, interpretation is conceived broadly enough so as to include human feeling responses to various signs and symbols, emotions as well as conceptions.

This book is not, however, about Peirce or philosophical theories of the imagination, despite the relevance of such matters to my theme. I develop no separate, elaborate apology for the semiotic perspective adopted here. (To a certain extent, the proof is in the pudding.) Nor do I argue that it is necessarily superior to or incompatible with other approaches to my topic. Nevertheless, I do want to contend that this perspective is uniquely adapted to the purpose of exposing the true nature of boredom as a problem of interpretation, a semiotic breakdown or incapacity.

The writing of this book is motivated by a single, simple observation: in certain instances, boredom *matters*. People do, in fact, become bored with relationships and activities that they continue to care a great deal about. Musicians become bored with their music, athletes with their competition, while never abandoning these activities, and a strong love can survive the boredom that might afflict a marriage or friendship. It is only in such instances that boredom constitutes a problem or crisis for the person experiencing it, and becomes a source of anxiety. Of course, I *can* be bored without its mattering very much to me (as when my interest fails to be engaged by the magazine that I am perusing in a physician's waiting room). But if I care about X and I am bored with X, then my situation is potentially troublesome, and this, I am suggesting, is the case for at least some persons whose religious lives lack intellectual and emotional intensity.

Boredom can matter from a certain third-person perspective as well. Indeed, it is just such a perspective that informs the traditional theological evaluation of acedia as a form of sinfulness. Generally speaking, my boredom can matter to someone else whether it matters to me or not. Others may conclude, for example, that there is something wrong with me if I am bored by a certain film or novel, or that it is important for me to take interest in my children's schoolwork or in recent political events. Ethical or aesthetic judgments articulated in the form of a claim that "you really ought to be interested in X" represent evaluations both of the object of my boredom and of that boredom itself. Given that the former is something that I "ought" to find meaningful, the latter is problematic.

Some readers might be a bit confused about what I mean by "meaning" when I use that word within the context of these deliberations. A few remarks may help to clarify my usage, without altogether dissolving the vagueness that, I think, necessarily and appropriately attaches to such a term. I do not invoke the term here in the narrow sense employed by analytic philosophers, such that "meaning" is construed solely as a property of sentences, with all other references to meaning being regarded as vacuous or nonsense. I confess that my usage is more akin to that of the old-fashioned existentialist philosophers. Meaning, even when it cannot be perfectly articulated or expressed, is a fundamental desideratum in human experience. Lacking it, human beings become bored, anxious, depressed. The search for it motivates much of human behavior. But this "it" is not some object or thing (despite what some persons might think or some advertisers might profess); rather, it has the character of a semiotic relationship. Concrete things can become a source of meaning insofar as they function as signs, precisely because meaning itself is a product and function of semiosis.

Perhaps it is more appropriate, then, to characterize my perspective on meaning (once again) as semiotic rather than purely existentialist. On that view, meaning is to be regarded as a characteristic of interpretive activity (embodied in what Peirce called "interpretants"). Human beings are engaged in a continuous process of interpreting signs, discovering their meaning, creating new signs. When that process is successful, human experience is charged with meaning. But such "success" can be construed in a great variety of ways, and meaningful interpretations are not to be restricted to those that can be verbally formulated in sentences.

THIS BOOK consists of five chapters:

The first chapter supplies a conceptual map, representing an attempt to situate the word *boredom* within an appropriate semantic field of synonyms, near-synonyms, and closely related terms. The primary goal of this chapter is to characterize boredom as religiously significant. Toward this end, I draw upon a diverse but carefully limited selection of philosophical, theological, and literary materials, ranging from Aquinas's reflections on the problem of acedia, through Dante's "dark wood" and John of the Cross's "dark night," to William James's considerations of the "sick soul." My survey emphasizes Christian perspectives, with a glance at related Jewish, Hindu, and Buddhist teachings. Despite the family resemblances, it is not my intention to ignore the various and important distinctions among the concepts represented on my "map." Nor is the title of chapter 1 designed to suggest that Aquinas's perspective is somehow normative for my account. Nevertheless, the ancient and medieval discussions of acedia as a "deadly sin" do provide an especially useful starting point for an inquiry concerning the religious significance of boredom.

In chapter 2, I extend this account to strategies for alleviating or avoiding boredom. A number of philosophers, perceiving boredom as symptomatic of a deeper existential condition that can be disguised but not readily transformed, reject such strategies as quite common but nevertheless foolish attempts at *diversion*. Pascal, Kierkegaard, and Heidegger are included in this group of thinkers and they all merit some attention here. At the same time, I consider the related but not identical problem of *distraction*. It is a commonplace that bored persons are typically and readily distracted. In certain instances this fact could be regarded as unimportant, but for someone engaged seriously in the practice of prayer, meditation, or ritual devotion, distraction can represent the most worrisome sort of obstacle. I compare the advice about prayer offered to Jewish and Christian practitioners with suggestions gleaned from some of the Buddhist literature on the cultivation of mindfulness.

Chapter 3 focuses on two types of prescriptive discourse: one encountered in treatises on the spiritual life (from a great variety of religious traditions), counseling the devotee to foster a certain sense of detachment or indifference regarding self and world (sometimes extending, paradoxically, even to the object of devotion itself); the other, in aesthetics, recommending an attitude of disinterestedness as a necessary precondition for experiencing any artwork as beautiful. I am convinced that these prescriptions have a distinctive logic, despite the puzzling form that they sometimes take.[4] And while neither religious indifference nor aesthetic disinterestedness can be identified with boredom pure and simple, I suggest that these phenomena (conceived at an appropriate level of vagueness) are all related; my purpose is to expose and describe the continuities among them.

The fourth chapter begins with an application of some basic elements of information theory to various religious ritual and meditative practices. Insofar as they are characterized by a high degree of redundancy, the risk of boredom for practitioners is a genuine one. But the fact that such ritual behavior can produce ecstatic as well as boring experiences is intriguing and deserves analysis. Here the role of redundancy in habit formation is examined. At the same time, I investigate the role of the imagination in both the production and the discovery of meaning. There is a complicated story to be told about the relationship between habit and the imagination. Habit represents a constraint on the possible, while the imagination is possibility's playground. To the degree that boredom is an experience of meaninglessness it might signal a failure of the imagination, resulting when the latter yields to the deadening effects of habit. Yet the gentle force of habit also empowers the imagination in ways that it is important to describe.

I supply the bulk of such a description in chapter 5, where my primary objective is to sketch a more thoroughly detailed semiotic of boredom. On my account, religiously meaningful experiences can be analyzed as semiotic events, events that are shaped, informed, even partially constituted by specific habits of thought and feeling. Such habits may actually induce boredom; yet they sometimes function as interpretive skills essential for the recognition of anything as having a religious meaning or sacred quality. Various spiritual exercises are intended to develop such skill, practices that serve both to stimulate and to discipline the imagination. This is the sort of skill utilized in the "discernment of spirits," a task for which Ignatius of Loyola formulated careful guidelines in his *Spiritual Exercises*. Jonathan Edwards was preoccupied with the same task, couching his analysis in explicitly semiotic terms, as it appears in the *Treatise on Religious Affections*. My purpose here is to suggest, rather than to demonstrate at any great length, how both of these texts can be regarded from a distinctively Peircean perspective.[5] The logic of indifference, previously analyzed in terms of Peirce's theory of abduction, is a logic that can now be conceived as semiotic.

I conclude these deliberations with a postlude, consisting in a brief meditation on waiting. Waiting can often be boring, so that the immediate relevance of this topic can be presented as a straightforward empirical observation. Here I want to probe the intuition that waiting is something that one can do poorly or do well, despite the fact that waiting appears not to be a matter of "doing" anything at all. Indeed, a variety of theological perspectives suggest that a certain capacity for waiting is of inestimable religious value, and something that can be developed through practice. These remarks are intended to underscore the character of waiting as a spiritual practice.

IT WOULD likely be perceived, at best, as ironic, at worst, as foolhardy to write a very long book about boredom. Reading very long books, like waiting in very long lines, can often help to precipitate the experience of boredom. Of course, the brevity of a work is no guarantee that, for any given individual, it will prove to be of interest. Nevertheless, I want to avoid the misconception that this book represents anything like an "exhaustive" account of its topic. Readers concerned with tracing the history of the concept of boredom are encouraged to look elsewhere.[6] Likewise, no one should expect to discover a good deal of practical advice in these pages about how one might best cope with or overcome chronic boredom. Rather, these are the reflections, neither purely random nor systematic, of a philosopher in midlife, one who, having confronted the "demon of noontide," felt an odd compulsion to think out loud about this encounter.[7] If the human experience of boredom is ubiquitous (as it appears to be), and if boredom matters (at least in some instances), then perhaps that compulsion is not so very odd, and no further apologetic for this discussion is required.

1

PORTRAYING ACEDIA

I T MAY seem inadequate, even misleading, to translate traditional discourse about acedia into a contemporary idiom organized around talk about boredom, even a spiritual boredom that characterizes and afflicts persons engaged in various religious practices. Such experiences of boredom, of spiritual "desolation," of "dryness" in prayer (including but not limited to the extreme condition depicted by mystics as the soul's "dark night") are carefully distinguished by some scholars from the sin of acedia.[1] The key issue here seems to be precisely the fact that acedia is a sin—indeed, one of the "seven deadly sins" in the Christian tradition. Temporary feelings of joylessness or desolation are an inevitable part of the spiritual life; these feelings are perceived by most theologians as playing an important, even necessary role in our spiritual economies. They are properly to be regarded as sinful, however, only to the extent that one is responsible for them or demonstrates no real concern about overcoming them. For example, spiritual boredom may result from an individual's failure to engage, with vigor and consistency, in appropriate spiritual exercises. Such a condition may persist to the extent that an individual makes no effort to alleviate it. Here it is appropriate to speak of acedia.

This sort of plea for greater precision in usage and translation deserves a carefully considered response. I am perfectly willing to admit at the outset that acedia, like the French word *ennui,* can be rendered into English as "boredom" only at the expense of a significant loss in meaning. At the same time, "boredom" seems a better translation than the typical usage of "sloth" for this purpose; idleness or laziness, like drowsiness, represents one of the "daughters" of acedia, but ought not to be identified with its essence.[2] The increased tendency, dating from the late medieval period, to understand acedia as sloth, focusing on external behavior and the sinner's idleness, represents a transformation and, in my evaluation, an impoverishment of the earlier conception. Aquinas, for example, clearly perceived acedia as consisting in a certain kind of joylessness, inappetence, a lack of interest in spiritual goods.

Now I take boredom, vaguely understood, to imply just such a lack of interest. It would seem inconsistent for someone to say "*X* is of great interest to me" and, at the same time, "I am bored with *X.*" Perhaps the translation of acedia as "boredom" seems to represent a trivializing of the concept, just as ennui for the French is not simply any kind of boredom, but a boredom tinged with deep melancholy. It is true that I can be bored by a great many things without anyone considering it to be a matter of tremendous consequence. But if I am bored with my career, or my marriage, or as in Aquinas's case with spiritual goods, then it is not so trivial a state of affairs. This is just to point out that the word *boredom* may have a greater range of extension, and a fuzzier connotation, than the term *acedia*. That fact can be compensated for through the use of appropriately descriptive adjectives, like "spiritual" or "chronic."

There is a deeper issue that intersects with the problem of appropriate translation. At the heart of the matter is the question of how the phenomenon of acedia is finally to be understood. I want to warn against the assumption that this question is an easy one to answer. The pursuit of an answer, it seems to me, points toward the very core of the spiritual life. Aquinas judged acedia to be the opposite of taking joy in the divine good, such joy comprising an essential ingredient of caritas, of the love of God.[3] That is why acedia was such serious business for the medieval theologians, representing a fundamental spiritual disorder. And serious matters deserve serious consideration.

Consider again that the primary distinction between acedia and spiritual dryness seems to be the fact that I am not directly responsible for the latter; only the former is a notion that has a decisively moral significance. Yet it is quite clear that acedia and spiritual dryness both share a number of important characteristics: a dulling of sensibilities, a lack of interest in spiritual

13

exercises, an intellectual and emotional sluggishness. The description of one state is not readily distinguishable from a description of the other; the key to making such a distinction lies in isolating the specific causes and effects of each phenomenon. This is not necessarily always a simple task. I will frame that task as a set of questions and translate it into the more general terms that I have been employing: To what extent am I responsible for feelings of boredom? What do I do in response to those feelings? Is my boredom something under my control or does it afflict me like a disease? What, if anything, does my boredom signify?

I want to argue here, among other things, that boredom may indicate the lack of a capacity to discern the full significance of a thing or situation. If "ought implies can," then it might seem possible to infer from this argument the claim that one is never responsible in such instances for one's bored condition. That inference would be mistaken, however, since one might be judged responsible for the task of developing the very capacity in question. If I neglect my training, I may then be unable to compete effectively in an athletic event. But certainly this is a state of affairs that I could have and perhaps should have prevented. Generally speaking, the sort of person that I am delimits my range of possible actions and perceptions. I can do only what is possible, yet to the extent that I control the sort of person that I am and will become, I partially define and determine these possibilities. So, too, with religious insight and the growth in religious knowledge. It takes practice.

14

I am not suggesting that boredom *always* signifies the lack of a certain perceptual skill or capacity. One may be perfectly able but nevertheless unwilling to perceive the significance of some thing or event. I might fail to see not because I am "blind" but rather because I simply choose to "close my eyes." This choice may be judged, in any particular instance, as a stubborn refusal to recognize the value of a thing or as the quite natural and inevitable result of fatigue. Moreover, I do not intend to suggest that one has such complete control over the development of one's physical, intellectual and spiritual capacities that the lack of some capacity always implies failure resulting from lack of effort. No matter how hard I might train, I cannot run a sub-four-minute mile.

The experience of boredom can signal either the absence of some meaningful object of perception or my failure to attend to it. I want to argue that this "failure to attend" is not so simple a matter as it might appear on the surface, so that the attribution of fault can quickly become murky. I regard the genesis of meaning as a complex semiotic event, an event shaped by the perceiver's powers of attention, understanding, and imagination, as well as by the presence and the nature of what is perceived. It is an event in which it makes sense to say that meaning is both produced and discovered. One of my goals in this discussion is to supply a reasonably clear sketch of some of the conditions that tend to preclude or distort such "meaning events." To the extent that persons exercise some control over these conditions, boredom can be perceived as a morally meaningful concept.[4] But my "interest" in boredom is not exhausted by its moral dimension. And the continuities between acedia and various other forms of spiritual dryness and disinterest are significant enough that my analysis of the former concept should be expected to shed light on a broad range of related phenomena. At least that is what these preliminary remarks are intended to suggest.

TALK ABOUT acedia as a "deadly sin" is one strand of traditional Christian discourse concerning the moral life. Nevertheless, it would be a mistake to assume that the problem of spiritual boredom is one over which Christians exercise exclusive property rights. Indeed, this Christian discourse itself is fully intelligible only when read against the backdrop supplied by the cultures of ancient Hellenism and the Near East.[5] Jewish warnings about the dangers of slothfulness bear an especially important relationship to later Christian teachings. The Hebrew Bible alone contains innumerable warnings of this sort, many of which appear in the wisdom literature. The apocryphal work Ecclesiasticus identifies laziness as the source of much evil (33:27), and Proverbs describes the ideal wife as one who avoids idleness (31:27). Narratives in the Hebrew Bible portray various individuals who, much like Jesus' disciples in Gethsemane, are overwhelmed by drowsiness and fall into a spiritually problematic sleep. These stories depict the sometimes disastrous consequences of a failure to pay attention, of a lack of moral vigilance, as in the famous case of Samson's downfall (Judges 16). For the Hebrew prophets, generally speaking, sin quite typically takes the form of a numbing indifference to the will of God. They constantly prod Israel with cautions about such apathy, a hardness of heart resulting in spiritual deafness and blindness, an inability to perceive the word of God.[6] The prophetic literature also supplies the most powerful images of an extreme acedia (although these images are multivalent and clearly able to support alternative interpretations). Consider, as two examples, Ezekiel's sojourn in the valley of the "dry bones" (in Ezekiel 37) and Isaiah's description of spiritually dead men who "stumble at noon as in the twilight" (Isaiah 59:10).

Sleep is employed as a metaphor for the dulling of spiritual awareness by various postbiblical Jewish thinkers. Among the Hasidim, Rabbi Nahman of Bratslav represents one notable case in point. For Nahman, the essential purpose of his religious teaching was to awaken "those human beings who have fallen asleep and sleep away their days."[7] Twentieth-century theologians influenced by Hasidism display the same sort of perspective, most especially in their talk about the true meaning of prayer as *kavanah*.[8] Boredom can either signify or cause the failure to pay attention, while *kavanah* is best understood as a loving "attentiveness to God." Much more than an emotional quality that attaches to prayer, it is rather a turning of the whole person—heart, mind, body, and soul—toward God in complete devotion. In stark contrast to the var-

17

ious ways in which bored individuals manage to "pass time" or "kill time," prayer with *kavanah* "is a crucible in which time is cast in the likeness of the eternal."[9]

Within the Hindu tradition, the Yoga Sutras of Patanjali identify *styāna* (translated variously as "apathy," "lack of enthusiasm," or "languor") and *ālasya* ("sloth," "laziness," or "lethargy") as the consequences of a failure to concentrate properly. These represent "distractions," serious obstacles to enlightenment.[10] Indeed, commentators on this sutra describe sloth as the "great enemy" of the religious aspirant, weakening the heart with cowardice and the body with sickness and fatigue, while plaguing the mind with doubts. Moderation in diet, wakefulness, and a gentle persistence in the practice of yoga are the best treatment for this condition of slothfulness. The enemy seeks to discourage; but even in periods haunted by dullness and distraction, spiritual progress is possible.[11]

In a similar fashion, Buddhist texts speak of the *nivarana* or "five hindrances," all of which cloud the mind and impede progress in the spiritual life.[12] "Sloth and torpor" (*thina-middha*), third among the items on this list, are described as negative dispositions that affect not only the intellect, but emotions and sense perceptions as well. Caused by feelings of discontent, mental sluggishness, laziness, poor posture, or excessive eating, sloth and torpor are strengthened by force of habit. Typically, they are manifested as drowsiness and an increased tendency to sleep. (This is both literally and metaphorically the case: the Buddha, as did Rabbi Nahman, described the effective presence of these hindrances as like being in a state of sleep.) They produce in the afflicted consciousness a quality of unwieldiness, of stiffness.[13] In colorful language, the slothful mind is depicted as being "inert as a bat hanging to a tree, or as molasses cleaving to a stick, or as a lump of butter too stiff for spreading."[14] It is also evoked by the image of water covered with mosses. Just as nothing can be reflected and perceived in water covered by plants, so too, the slothful mind is unable to discern its own true nature, thus, unable to achieve liberating insight.

Here, the dispositional character of sloth, its various physical manifestations, and its negative status as an obstacle to religious awareness are all themes that link Buddhist and Christian reflections on this topic. At the same time, one discovers in the Buddhist concept of *sunyata*, as well as in the world-weariness of Ecclesiastes,[15] a powerful vision of the emptiness of all things, something akin to a deep boredom, but acting to stimulate rather than cloud awareness. Likewise, within Christianity, acedia is to be resisted, but the achievement of a certain kind of disinterestedness is regarded as necessary for real progress in the spiritual life. Clearly, then, it is important to distinguish between good and bad species of indifference, a task of discernment to which all of the religious traditions discussed here devote considerable attention, and one to which I will return frequently in my own ruminations.

Saint Thomas Aquinas's discussion of acedia appears in the second part of his *Summa Theologica*, but this medieval notion has roots that run deep in the Christian tradition. Regarding the New Testament sources, Jesus' gentle admonition of his disciples in Gethsemane pales by comparison with the much sharper condemnation of spiritual apathy recorded in the third chapter of Revelations: "I know your works: you are neither cold nor hot. Would that you were cold or hot! So, because you are lukewarm, and neither cold nor hot, I will spew you out of my mouth."

Extended theological reflection concerning acedia begins during the fourth century of the common era. Evagrius took special pains to warn his brother monks about the "demon of noontide," a powerful boredom that "besieges" the devotee, resulting in distraction from, sometimes even abandonment of, the spiritual life.[16] The only appropriate response to such an attack is a disciplined persistence in spiritual exercises—prayer, meditation, the reading of scripture, and the like—while steadfastly resisting the inclination toward restlessness, sleepiness, and, ultimately, despair. Manual labor was also considered by Evagrius and his contemporaries to be an important weapon in the monk's spiritual arsenal, especially since laziness or "sloth" was recognized as one of acedia's chief byproducts, and thus symptomatic of the enemy's success.

With his heavy use of martial images and vocabulary, Evagrius represents a strand of Christian spirituality that can be traced back to the Gospels and Saint Paul, while extending up to and beyond Saint Ignatius of Loyola in the sixteenth century. Here the individual's experience of boredom is perceived as the work of evil spirits, in effect, a summons to spiritual combat. Of course, in order to engage the enemy, one must first be able to recognize him as such. Good soldiers, like good athletes, know how to "read the signs" that betray an enemy's or opponent's intentions. This is no less important in spiritual combat than in human warfare. Indeed, in the former case, interpretive skill is of special value, since the stakes of the contest are so high (eternal life) and the opponent is one possessing supernatural power. Clearly, then, the martial context that Evagrius invoked presupposes rather than precludes the semiotic framework that I am recommending as felicitous for understanding boredom.

In the spiritual life, boredom is an important sign, but I want to propose that it is not always an unambiguous one. Even from this martial perspective, dryness and disinterest are quite frequently but not exclusively perceived as the effects wrought by an evil spirit. Moreover, the experience of great spiritual joy, typically one of the positive fruits of prayer, may instead constitute evidence of the enemy's clever strategy, a temptation to complacence and spiritual pride.

In talking about acedia, Evagrius and the desert fathers employed a term whose history of usage in the Greek displays its own considerable vagueness.[17] Meaning literally a "lack of care," the word could have a positive or a negative connotation, positive in those instances when "care" might represent some troublesome psychic burden. Correspondingly, the feeling of "not caring" is itself a vague sign, interpretable either as something actively to be resisted or to be cultivated. (Such vagueness might help to account for the puzzling, seemingly paradoxical nature of the petition in T. S. Eliot's poem "Ash Wednesday," where he prays, "Teach us to care and not to care. Teach us to sit still.")[18]

Nevertheless, for Evagrius and the Christian tradition that he helped to shape, the word *acedia* had a decisively negative connotation and the experience that it identifies was one to be eschewed. The more positive sense in which one can be lacking in care, can be passionless or disinterested, comes to be denoted by the word *apatheia*. Again, it is Evagrius who constitutes an important source of early Christian reflection on *apatheia*: he regarded it as an essential precondition for genuine charity.[19] In contrast to the victim of acedia, an individual possessing this virtue will be able to pray without distraction, enjoying a peaceful state of mind, in control of and so undisturbed by all sensations, thoughts, and feelings. Such an individual is "free" to love God.

Here the element of control seems crucial. This is a cultivated boredom, one that arises as a conditioned response to carefully specified objects and only as those objects are framed in a particular fashion (as leading the devotee away from rather than toward God). The word *boredom* stretches to the breaking point here, because none of the agitation, restlessness, or anxiety that we typically associate with that psychic state is properly descriptive of *apatheia*. But the vagueness of the term can be mitigated by appropriate qualifiers; this is "good" boredom, a "practiced" disinterest in ephemeral goods, not a vice, but rather, a mark of spiritual progress.

22

John Cassian was largely responsible for mediating Evagrian teachings about acedia to the West. But on his account, acedia increasingly becomes identified with one of its offspring, laziness or idleness.[20] Focusing less on the subjective experience of spiritual boredom or apathy, and more on its physical manifestation as drowsiness or laziness, Cassian recommended manual labor as the principal remedy for this affliction, and understood "fortitude" to be the virtue most directly opposed to this vice.

The conception of acedia as sloth was to become the dominant one at a much later point in time. But during the intervening medieval period, the term retained a greater psychological depth of meaning, being construed as a designation for spiritual boredom, depression, a lack of interest in spiritual goods and exercises.[21] It is within this medieval context that Aquinas articulated his own views on the sin of acedia. He described it as an "oppressive sorrow," a mental "sluggishness" afflicting a person so that "he wants to do nothing."[22] It is a special kind of sorrow (*tristitia*) that has as its object the divine good, as such, directly opposed to the joy (*guadium*) that springs from the love of God.

For Aquinas, sorrow in itself is not blameworthy. The special nature of acedia as "sorrow for the divine good" is what constitutes it as a vice. The person who experiences and consents to such sorrow is guilty of violating the third commandment, the precept concerning the Sabbath that Aquinas interpreted as a command both to rest and to delight in God's presence.[23] Such a person rejects the end for which God created human beings, the joyful union with God that is effected and sustained by love.

Of course, the issue of consent is an important one insofar as any judgment of sinfulness is concerned. Even holy men, Aquinas admitted, experience "imperfect movements" of acedia, "but they do not reach to the consent of reason."[24] Acedia cannot be reduced to a passion, then, but involves also a necessary element of volition, a decision to indulge in or to resist certain feelings of sorrow. As I have already remarked, this element of volition is what distinguishes acedia as a sin from the occasional and altogether inevitable experience of spiritual dryness. It is not that these experiences themselves are remarkably different; both might be described as cases of spiritual boredom. It is what one chooses to do with the experience, so to speak, that seems to make the moral difference for Aquinas.

Some vices, like fornication, are to be overcome by flight, but the key to defeating acedia, for Aquinas just as for Evagrius and Cassian, is resistance. One afflicted with this spiritual sorrow is encouraged to persevere in prayer and meditation, precisely because "the more we think about spiritual goods, the more pleasing they become to us." Since the divine good is infinitely pleasing in itself, it offers the best hope of a cure for this disorder. Besieged by boredom and distraction, the mind should hold fast to the object of its contemplation, its loving gaze sustained by a confidence that joy and peace must eventually be restored. From a certain contemporary perspective, variety may be considered as the "spice of life," but for Aquinas persistence is the key to overcoming spiritual boredom.

Failure to persist has serious consequences on Aquinas's account, as he follows the earlier tradition in listing among the "daughters" of acedia, idleness, drowsiness, uneasiness of the mind, restlessness of the body, curiosity, loquacity, and despair. His analysis suggests that boredom is both an impediment and a stimulus to action. While it manifests itself as a weariness, a sluggishness in the performance of spiritual exercises, acedia also induces the mind to pursue certain distractions, often in the form of sensual pleasures that appear to offer relief from the burden of sorrow. Here Aquinas helps to expose one of the peculiar characteristics of boredom as a psychic state; namely, that while the bored person "wants to do nothing," she is often driven frantic with the doing of many things.

Aquinas's analysis would seem to accord a certain primacy to despair among the daughters of acedia. The spiritual goods to which this sin represents an aversion can be classified either as an end or as a means.[25] Sluggishness in responding to the commandments is an example of the latter, a slothful neglecting of those goods that serve as means to an end. But despair represents a shunning of the very end of the spiritual life, a consequence of the refusal to love God devotedly, to rejoice in the divine goodness (what Kierkegaard was much later to call the "sickness unto death").

Acedia finds representation in the poetry as well as the theology of the Middle Ages. It is perhaps ironic

25

that Dante's encounter with those souls being purged of the sin of acedia, in canto XVIII of the *Purgatorio*, has the effect of suddenly dispelling his own drowsiness. Like Aquinas, Dante portrayed acedia as a phenomenon of defective love. These sinners were guilty not simply of apathy in the pursuit of spiritual exercises, narrowly conceived, but more generally of a "lukewarmness in well-doing." Now they must endure a fitting punishment, being filled with a constant "desire to keep moving" so that they cannot rest. They have lost the ability to pray, but they cry out poignantly, "Haste, haste, lest time be lost for little love, that zeal in well-doing may make grace come green again."[26]

Dante's poetic narrative commences "in the middle of the journey of life" when, far removed from either the innocent enthusiasm of youth or the serene wisdom of old age, he is himself most vulnerable to the noontide demon. His drowsiness in purgatory mirrors the earlier sleepiness that threatened to overtake him while he wandered lost in the dark wood, at the very beginning of the *Inferno*. Indeed, a much darker image of acedia, in its most terrifying and fully developed form, appears in canto VII of the *Inferno*, as Dante and Vergil penetrate the fifth circle of hell. There they discover souls completely vanquished by the enemy, drowned in their own despair even as they now lie sunken in the slime of the river Styx, gurgling their hymn, "We were sullen in the sweet air that is gladdened by the sun, bearing in our hearts a sluggish smoke (*accidioso fummo*); now we are sullen in the black mire."[27]

Less than a century after Dante, Chaucer offered another poetic depiction of the sin of acedia, in "The Parson's Tale." There he discourses at length on "accidie," a vice that makes a person "hevy, thoghtful, and wrawe." It "binimeth him the love of alle goonesse." "Accidie" works to "forsloweth and forsluggeth" the individual in his endeavors, eventuating in despair of God's mercy, or "wanhope." Ultimately, "it freseth al the herte of man," leaving him bitter and cold.[28]

Here some old insights are confirmed, but as the medieval period draws to a close, the use of the word *acedia* to communicate these insights becomes increasingly problematic.[29] Over the centuries, it had acquired such numerous and diverse connotations that its meaning was at risk of evaporating in a cloud of vagueness. In its continued usage, as I have already indicated, the word tended to be employed ever more narrowly as a designation for idleness and sloth. Of course, the experience of boredom, even in explicitly religious contexts, by no means disappeared with the waning of the Middle Ages. The Renaissance literature on "melancholy" supplied a new perspective on this spiritual lethargy, treating it more typically as a disease to be cured than as a sin to be resisted.[30]

"Melancholy," in its Renaissance usage, is certainly not conceived as an exclusively religious phenomenon. But the problem of spiritual boredom, variously designated, does continue to merit serious attention from theologians and spiritual writers in the postmedieval period. Consider, as one important example, Ignatius of Loyola's warnings about "desolation" in his *Spiritual*

Exercises. This condition is described as "darkness of soul, turmoil of spirit, inclination to what is low and earthly, restlessness rising from many disturbances and temptations which lead to want of faith, want of hope, want of love. The soul is wholly slothful, tepid, sad, and separated, as it were, from its Creator and Lord."[31]

It is of interest to note that while Ignatius did associate desolation with the workings of an "evil spirit," he enumerated three different reasons why one might be afflicted by such darkness.[32] The first reason involved one's negligence of "exercises of piety," and here Ignatius seemed to be describing acedia in the most traditional sense of that term. But the second and third reasons are of a markedly different character. In the second case, Ignatius warned, God may be employing desolation as a trial, in order "to see how much we are worth." The third and final reason why one might suffer from desolation is "because God wishes to give us a true knowledge of ourselves." The key ingredient of such self-knowledge is the awareness that spiritual joy or "consolation" is not something that one can manipulate. It is not the inevitable concomitant of engaging in a specific practice or contemplating a particular spiritual good. Rather, it is the gracious gift of God alone.

Following Ignatius's reasoning, one may experience desolation and be quite unable to do anything about it. Moreover, the religiously edifying point of such an experience consists precisely in recognizing the fact of one's impotence. There can be no investment strategy designed to guarantee spiritual joy as a return. There are no spiritual technologies that can produce consolation and prevent desolation. The good "soldier" must be ready to meet whatever it is that God or the enemy may send his way, discerning enough to know the difference, detached enough to love not what he chooses but what he finds.

Ignatius's logic of discernment, as it is to be applied to the experiences of consolation and desolation, deserves careful and extended consideration. But I want immediately to note the complexity of Ignatius's portrayal of spiritual desolation, a concept broad enough to accommodate traditional talk about acedia, yet with shades of meaning more akin to those that Saint John of the Cross evoked when he wrote about the "dark" but edifying trials that a soul must endure in its spiritual journey.

John devoted a good deal of effort to the tasks of describing and interpreting the "dark night of the soul." Indeed, his account is much more lengthy and detailed than that supplied by Ignatius in his brief remarks about desolation. Certain features of that account, however, are directly comparable to Ignatius's reflections. In the first book of his "The Dark Night," John warned about the "spiritual sloth" that is likely to distract beginners soon after their earliest successes in the spiritual life: "Since they are so used to finding delight in spiritual practices, they become bored when they do not find it. If they do not receive in prayer the satisfaction they crave—for after all it is fit that God withdraw this so as to try them—they do not want to return to it or at times they either give up prayer or go to it begrudgingly."[33]

Despite being framed by talk about slothfulness and vice, these remarks reveal that God may actually cause such darkness in the soul, much as Ignatius suggested, in order to test it. At this point, acedia and spiritual dryness seem indistinguishable. The individual can now choose to succumb to this condition (consent to it) or to resist it and persevere in the practice of prayer. In the former case, a continuing boredom with spiritual matters may be analyzed as the effect of slackness in religious exercises, a lack of devotion, a surrendering to distractions. Yet even the path of perseverance offers no guarantee that the experience of boredom will be quickly or easily dispelled. God may choose to leave these afflicted souls for a time in such "darkness" and "dryness" that "they do not know which way to turn in their discursive imaginings." No longer resulting in insight or in feelings of joy, meditation has now become "distasteful and bitter" for them.

John admits that sin may be the primary source of this aridity, not just a factor in sustaining it. That is to say, God is not always the cause of spiritual boredom and not all such experiences should be interpreted as a test, or as a method of purgation: "Because the origin of these aridities may not be the sensory night and purgation, but sin and imperfection, or weakness and luke-warmness, or some bad humor or bodily disposition, I will give some signs here for the discerning whether the dryness is the result of this purgation or of one of these other defects."[34] These remarks form the prelude to a semiotic analysis, as John proceeds to offer his own rules or "signs" for the discernment of spirits. Several signs serve to indicate when boredom might represent a God-given "test" of the soul's mettle. The first of these is when boredom extends to various sense objects and images; it is not confined to spiritual goods, but rather, the soul finds no pleasure or consolation in anything. The third sign has to do with repeated failure in meditation, a dramatic "breakdown" of the imagination. It is John's second sign, however, that is most immediately relevant to the task of portraying acedia in the narrower sense. It consists in the fact that a person suffering "purgative dryness" will be "pained about his not serving God." Such dryness differs from lukewarmness, because the lukewarm person will have "no solicitude about serving God." So in both instances a person experiences spiritual boredom; but it is only in the former instance that, for the person experiencing it, boredom really matters.

Recall that John identified three possible alternatives for the "origin of these aridities." In addition to human vice and the divine will, spiritual boredom may be linked to "some bad humor or bodily disposition" as its cause. This last possibility, boredom as a symptom of psychic and/or physical disease, is the primary perspective embodied in the Renaissance literature on melancholy. It also informs William James's treatment of this topic, in the sixth and seventh of his Gifford Lectures on religious experience.

James's "sick soul," in its most serious manifestations, represents a disorder so severe that it would appear to be a gross trivialization of that concept to identify such a person as "bored," without further qualification. This is an acutely self-conscious boredom that reduces the human psyche to a state of numb indifference, before plunging it into anxiety and despair. In its initial stages, it takes the form of "passive joylessness and dreariness, discouragement, dejection, lack of taste and zest and spring," a condition for which James borrowed the name *"anhedonia."*[35] In these earliest stages of the disease, it is an "incapacity for joyous feeling" that may later evolve into a "positive and active anguish."

James clearly did not share all of Aquinas's theological motivations or moral premises. But as we move from the thirteenth century to the dawn of the twentieth, certain lines of continuity emerge, connecting these otherwise disparate portrayals of the problem of spiritual boredom. For James as well as for Aquinas, the individual in question is one afflicted by a deep sorrow or melancholy, unable to experience joy or take interest. James had his own personal predilection for "the martial type of character."[36] He, too, understood it to be a matter of vital importance that the individual fight strenuously to overcome spiritual boredom, a task made especially complicated by the fact that this affliction almost always seems to involve a certain paralysis of the will. James even agreed with his more orthodox Christian predecessors that the renewal of "interest," the rebirth of meaning, is itself somewhat gratuitous. If not always to be credited as a gift from God, it is a "gift" nevertheless, "from sources sometimes high and sometimes low."[37] And so while the struggle to find meaning in life is an important one, that effort bears no simple relationship to the discovery of meaning as cause to effect.

William James's meditations on the sick soul expose certain features of that troubled psyche, however, that resonate more with the sort of existential "dis-ease" described by Pascal and Kierkegaard than with acedia. The victim of acedia has no taste for spiritual goods and religious exercises, but for the sick soul, quite literally, "nothing matters." The latter experiences a thorough-going "disenchantment with ordinary life" precipitated, at least to some extent, by the awareness that "back of everything is the great spectre of universal death, the all-encompassing blackness."[38] This dreadful state of mind is beautifully, hauntingly evoked by the poetry of Charles Baudelaire, in verses that repeatedly transport us to "the planes of *Ennui*, vacant and profound."[39] Samuel Beckett explored the same spiritual landscape in his plays and novels, portraying individuals for whom life has been reduced to a boring game, without joy, devoid of meaning. Such is the case in *Waiting for Godot*, where Vladimir is "bored to death"; he worries that "in an instant all will vanish and we'll be alone once more, in the midst of nothingness!"[40]

Here, again, no sharp division between the various species of spiritual boredom is necessary or even possible. Recall that John of the Cross had already identified a type of "aridity" that extends beyond spiritual goods, infecting a person's response to all created things. Moreover, I want to argue here that all significant experiences of boredom (acedia and all of its "cousins," if you will) have something to do with the awareness of death, the recognition that all things must pass away in time. Another way of putting this is to say that boredom has something to do with "nothing," the nothingness that lurks behind and threatens each person, every project, each moment. To make this sort of an argument will involve pressing beyond the immediate task of portraying boredom toward a deeper investigation of its various possible causes, conditions, and effects. I intend to delay that investigation only long enough to add a few details to my sketch (while organizing some details already presented).

BOREDOM SITS on a conceptual map somewhere between interest and despair. It clearly implies a lack of interest or meaning, and when that lack is serious enough, a person risks falling victim to feelings of meaninglessness, and even of despair. The more bored one becomes, the further away one moves from a state of being interested, the closer to despair.

Ennui is a term from the French that designates a boredom colored by melancholy. Acedia is a word with Greek roots that underscores the human responsibility for this psychic condition. On this view, boredom is a state of affairs that I ought to try to do something about. Acedia also points to the religious significance of boredom. It is a refusal of the joy that comes from the love of God. Indeed, at the heart of this theological conception of acedia is the understanding of boredom as a consequence of "too little love," an incapacity to love deeply.

Both as ennui and acedia, boredom is portrayed as a kind of sorrow or sadness, bordering on depression. Boredom has a broader, fuzzier connotation than these terms because I can be bored without it mattering to me or anyone else. But the person afflicted by ennui suffers greatly from this condition and is often the object of pity. With acedia, the bored person may be paralyzed by sloth, but nevertheless he *ought* to care about his condition, and others will judge him accordingly.

In some cases, the person experiencing ennui may be admired rather than pitied. This is the case if her suffering is deemed a noble suffering, a sign that she is superior to the things and people around her. That is to say, nothing is deemed worthy of her interest. People will often affect boredom for precisely this reason: to demonstrate their superiority with regard to certain persons, activities, situations. To be interested in something represents a form of dependence on that thing; I draw upon it as a source of enjoyment and satisfaction. I may judge that dependence to be unhealthy or unwarranted and so cultivate a certain disinterest in the thing. The motivation for this judgment may be arrogance, false pride. It may also be some kind of religious insight.

A certain power of discernment is required in order to distinguish between the vice of acedia and the desirable quality of *apatheia*. If something is perceived as an obstacle to progress in the spiritual life, then lacking interest in it might well be regarded as a positive state of affairs. Cultivating such disinterest could constitute an exercise in virtue formation. Of course, the same thing may be perceived as an obstacle in some respect or under certain conditions, but not so from another perspective. There is no simple formula for distinguishing between cases, but the discerning individual will not readily confuse the sin of acedia with a holy indifference (just as for the Buddhist, sloth and torpor are very far removed from the prescribed state of equanimity, of detachment). One relevant factor here is freedom, the sense of self-mastery that is characteristic of a virtuous indifference, but contrasts sharply with boredom, often manifested as the experience of being trapped, confined, and afflicted (like the desert monk in his cell).

A bored person is indifferent, disinterested, does not care. To be unconcerned about one's boredom is to be uninterested in one's own disinterest, to not care about not caring. My failure to find some event or activity interesting is the result of an interpretation. *Boredom is the result of semiosis.*[41] My decision to care or not to care about my own lack of interest itself rests upon an interpretation, this time with my boredom as its object. *Boredom is a sign.*

The pairing of boredom with depression defines a conceptual space that embraces ancient and medieval thinking about *tristitia*, French meditations on ennui (from Pascal to Baudelaire), Renaissance deliberations concerning melancholy, and William James's probing of the sick soul. The understanding of boredom as a kind of depression or disease may seem very far removed from any view of boredom as sin or vice. But on a carefully drawn map there will be no great distance marked between these conceptions. In the first place, my health—

physical, psychic, or spiritual—is something for which I am at least partially responsible. Boredom may be a disease that afflicts me because of my own negligence. (Here a moral "ought" is interjected.) On the other hand, nothing precludes the possibility of conceiving of sin as itself a kind of moral disease. Indeed, (whether it be judged as sinful or not) boredom (like yawning) often seems to be contagious.

The word *boredom* derives its meaning from its relationship to a diverse family of terms. Boredom implies drudgery, banality, lethargy, monotony, redundancy, tedium. Habit is often perceived as the mother of boredom. Being jaded is a species of boredom. A bored person experiences emptiness, listlessness, restlessness, drowsiness. Such a person often sleeps too much, talks too much, eats too much, seeks diversion, amusements, succumbs to distractions. Boredom resonates with torpor, languor, dullness, reduced awareness, insensitivity. We typically associate boredom with the landscape of the desert; with flatness, dryness, the color gray, midday, midlife; with tourists; with yawning. Boredom thwarts the spirit of play and signifies art's failure. Work may be boring but play is not supposed to be. Few comments are more damning of a work of art than "it is boring."

The bored person has a great deal of difficulty paying attention. Since meditation is, in a sense, the practice of paying attention, it is easy to understand why boredom is such an important problem in the spiritual life. I cannot truly love that to which I cannot fully attend, and so it is possible to regard the inattentiveness that characterizes boredom as a great threat to love. (Within Christian theology, acedia is portrayed as a sin against love.) Yet boredom does not preclude love and a strong love must be able to endure boredom.

Boredom can represent a failure of the imagination. Yet, as Kierkegaard realized, it can also be a powerful stimulus to the imagination. I can use my imagination to defeat boredom. My ability to do so, however, is not unequivocally a good thing. The imagination itself is perceived by spiritual writers both as an aid to religious insight and as a powerful source of distractions. Here, again, control is an important factor. The imagination is a powerful weapon, both in the devotee's spiritual arsenal, and in the devil's.

Boredom is a relational concept. The adjective "boring" misleads us into thinking that it is a property or quality of some thing, person, event, or activity. But any boring X is typically boring *to* or *for* someone, and under certain specifiable conditions. To pronounce oneself bored is to describe one's relationship to some thing or activity, in a given situation or environment. What is boring for one person may be of great interest to another. Once again, it is a matter of interpretation.

Boredom can afflict my relationship to a specific object. Nevertheless, at its deepest levels, boredom is an attitude that affects and infects my relationship to all possible objects. This sort of boredom is one that "I carry around with me" (like the bored tourist who fails to be engaged by anything on his itinerary). It cannot be eliminated simply by redirecting my attention or by removing a particular object that fails to interest me.

The failure is not in the object but in myself. The problem is dispositional.

Boredom can result either from having nothing to do or from being overwhelmed with things to do.[42] One can be bored doing many things. Yet there are no intrinsically boring situations. Boredom can represent either a necessary form of psychic rest or an empty restlessness. To be interested in everything, at all times and without exception, would very likely lead to madness. To be interested in nothing would very quickly lead to despair.

I may become bored when surrounded either by a great deal of noise or by silence. Busyness and leisure can both be invitations to boredom. But I will want to argue here that it is the boredom linked to silence and leisure that is more significant for the purpose of understanding the religious imagination.

I also argue that one can be bored without knowing it. This may seem, at first, like an implausible argument. But it is comparable to the claim that one might be angry or jealous without being fully conscious of the fact. Indeed, we often rely heavily on others to interpret our own psychic or spiritual states. Since it is all a matter of interpretation, it is reasonable to expect that I might fail to make the correct one.

For the person who is bored, *time* often seems to stand still. Cassian, in his reflections on the monastic life, noted the effect of boredom in producing altered perceptions of time. The German word for boredom, *Langweile*, quite literally conveys this temporal aspect of the experience. The bored person may work feverishly to fill time or "kill" time. But once seized by an over-powering boredom, time yawns a chasm that no activity or imagination can seem to fill. Indeed, the imagination is crucified by this experience of boredom, so that it must either choke and drown in despair or be altogether liberated from the burden of filling up time with images and things, awakened to the infinity of meaning that dwells in each thing, each moment.

2

KILLING TIME

STRATEGIES OF DIVERSION

Thoreau doubted that it is possible to "kill time without injuring eternity."[1] It is worth considering the source of his doubt, since the primary motivation for "killing time" would appear to be the desire to alleviate boredom. What fuels this desire? I want to propose one potential answer to this question: "killing time" is a rather futile form of self-defense, of self-preservation. One attempts to kill time because time inevitably kills all things, bringing the "death" of each moment, the death of all living beings. All things run their course and pass away, *in time.*

Now the strategies of diversion may sometimes be pursued instinctively, not always be explicitly mapped out. Diversion itself is a kind of forgetfulness, a fact that helps to explain both its futility and the nature of Thoreau's concern. It represents an attempt to "forget" about time and the inevitability of death, while nevertheless appearing as nothing more than an endeavor to escape the irritant of boredom. But boredom itself is a heightened awareness of the passing of time. Lacking any immediate object of interest or enjoyment, the bored person is left alone with time. Ironically, this condition is one typically described with the language of plenitude. Such persons have time on their hands—too much time with nothing to do. Time stretches interminably for the bored person, seems never-ending. This is empty time, however, dead time—just as the individual who must endure it feels hollow and lifeless. The bored person has plenty of nothing, and it is this heightened awareness of nothingness that makes chronic boredom so intolerable. Therein lies an important motivation for seeking diversion, amusement. At the same time, the cost of doing so is clear: forgetfulness, a diminution of awareness.

It will be important to assess this cost. After all, some things are regarded as best forgotten and heightened awareness is not always a self-evidently worthy goal. (The reader can combat boredom here by generating examples to illustrate the point.) Indeed, the sort of awareness that I have associated with boredom—of time passing, of the emptiness of experience, of nothingness—seems likely, if unmitigated, to eventuate in despair. Why cultivate such a psychic condition? Why warn about those diversionary tactics that help to relieve this condition?

Here it might be important to distinguish between the various forms and degrees of boredom. In certain instances, when the experience of boredom is both rather trivial and clearly temporary (as in the physician's waiting room or the long checkout line in a grocery store), attempts at simple diversion may be judged quite harmless, even laudatory, if they demonstrate a certain liveliness of imagination. From a religious point of view, this judgment will vary depending on a number of factors, including the value ascribed to some immediate object of attention, the perceived spiritual maturity of the person being judged (children are less likely than adults to be condemned for failure to attend), and the extent to which a given religious tradition advocates the cultivation of mindfulness as a continuous, ongoing spiritual practice.

There is another type of boredom, however, deeper and more persistent—one that is capable of inspiring a frantic search for diversion, for something to do. I have already described it as dispositional, affecting an individual's habits of feeling, thought, and perception so that he is incapable of finding and enjoying meaning in circumstances where it is judged that he ought. Acedia represents one form of this incapacity, where the "ought" has significant moral connotations (this condition is deemed to be one that could have been resisted, perhaps prevented). In other instances, the attribution of fault cannot be so readily made. In these cases, the "ought" is softer, translatable as "most people would" or "should if she could." Here it is recognized that the inability to "take interest" is a state of affairs that may lie beyond a particular person's control. What distinguishes all of the relevant cases from a simpler, more trivial form of disinterest is the chronic quality of the boredom experienced. This is a boredom that haunts and lingers.

It is just such a profound boredom that Pascal had in mind when he described the wretchedness of the human condition as consisting in "inconstancy, boredom, anxiety."[2] Moreover, for Pascal, the primary source of this wretchedness is the awareness, quite frequently obscured, that one exists suspended between the "two abysses of infinity and nothingness." As rational creatures, we emerge from the void of nonbeing only to contemplate an infinity that reduces us to nothingness: "For, after all, what is man in nature? A nothing compared to the infinite, a whole compared to the nothing, a middle point between all and nothing, infinitely remote from an understanding of the extremes."[3]

If we think our way backward in time we eventually encounter an incomprehensible nothingness, not only our own nonexistence but, pushing back further still, the nonexistence of all created things. If we project ourselves forward, we confront the inevitable darkness of death. If we stand in the present moment and look outward, we survey the empty infinity of space. If we shift our gaze inward we perceive the nullity of a self reduced to infinitesimal smallness by the vast All. Such is the human condition on Pascal's account, so that only a "supernatural torpor" could cause a person to be indifferent or insensitive to the magnitude of his predicament.[4]

Nevertheless, it is in just such a state of torpor that

most persons exist, preoccupying themselves with trivial matters, distracting themselves from the wretchedness of their lives, as well as from the inexorable approach of death. "*Diversion.* Being unable to cure death, wretchedness and ignorance, men have decided, in order to be happy, not to think about such things. But take away their diversion and you will see them bored to extinction. Then they feel their nullity without realizing it, for nothing could be more wretched than to be intolerably depressed as soon as one is reduced to introspection with no means of diversion."[5]

Here, in short formula, is Pascal's conception of the true nature of boredom: a feeling of "nullity without realizing it." Consider, first, that boredom is a feeling. To pronounce oneself bored is to report about the way that one feels. In a Peircean fashion, I regard feelings as vague thoughts that represent an interpretive response to some thing or situation. But a feeling may itself invite or even require interpretation. Pascal makes this point when he identifies boredom as a feeling that one can have "without realizing it." Determining what and how I feel is not a matter of simple introspection. Rather, I may best discern my true feelings by observing how they are manifested in and shape my actual behavior. With boredom, my attempt to mask or elude it through diversion is evidence of its presence. Even my verbal behavior can display this masking strategy as "I am bored" becomes transformed into "it is boring." The feeling of boredom is projected onto some object. My failure to take interest becomes the object's failure to interest me. The solution to boredom becomes a search for new objects of potential interest, the restless search for diversion.

I may fail to "realize" my boredom because I am engaged in pursuing various strategies of diversion. Yet Pascal argued that this failure can persist even when my diversions have been eliminated. Then I may feel my boredom but not recognize its true essence; that is, not recognize it as a "feeling of nullity." Failing to probe the depths of my experience of boredom, I misinterpret it as the simple absence of diversion. So whether the feeling is numbed by some actual amusement or acute in the absence of any such preoccupation, I fail to understand what my boredom is all about.

Now this failure to understand, to realize the true nature of boredom, however characteristic of the human condition on Pascal's account, is by no means inevitable. It is the very possibility of learning what our boredom has to teach us that makes this experience so potentially significant, at the same time, underscoring the danger of diversion. "The only thing that consoles us for our miseries is diversion. And yet it is the greatest of our miseries. It is that above all which prevents us from thinking about ourselves and leads us imperceptibly to destruction. But for that we should be bored, and boredom would drive us to seek some more solid means of escape, but diversion passes our time and brings us imperceptibly to our death."[6]

What, precisely, is the "more solid means of escape" to which Pascal here alludes? Elsewhere, he suggested that the instinct to seek diversion is opposed in human nature by another, and more noble, instinct—namely, the impulse to find our true happiness in a state of "rest." This instinct is, for Pascal, a vestige of the "greatness of our original nature." Nevertheless, in our present state of "confusion," we conflate one instinct with the other, assuming that our diversions will bring us the satisfaction that we most desire: "All our life passes in this way: we seek rest by struggling against certain obstacles, and once they are overcome, rest proves intolerable because of the boredom it produces. We must get away from it and crave excitement."[7]

The problem with boredom is that, as a painful irritant, it can inspire elaborate strategies of diversion, resulting in a frenzy of misguided activity. More positively, it can signal, for the properly discerning individual, the folly of all such plans of action and so, indirectly, a "more solid means of escape." If boredom is an experience of emptiness, it is nevertheless a meaningful emptiness on Pascal's account, and one that he was inclined to interpret in explicitly religious terms. "What else does this craving, and this helplessness, proclaim but that there was once in man a true happiness, of which all that now remains is the empty print and trace? This he tries in vain to fill with everything around him, seeking in things that are not there the help he cannot find in those that are, though none can help, since this infinite abyss can be filled only with an infinite and immutable object; in other words, by God himself."[8]

Like Augustine, Pascal perceived the Deity as supplying for the restless human heart its ultimate and only true resting place. This is a restfulness, a peace, that all human beings crave but no humanly contrived plan of action can secure. It is a divine gift that must be embraced in faith, a faith precluded by the individual's inability to confront boredom, endure boredom, perceive it as a sign, and so learn the painful lesson that it has to teach. The impulse to suppress boredom, to seek some instant or immediate pleasure, is a powerful one, in Pascal's view, most especially so because of our blinded, fallen condition. To act on this impulse is an exercise in futility. Moreover, for Pascal as well as for Thoreau, it represented a form of self-deception, a dangerous and contrived forgetfulness. Bored individuals frantically struggle to kill time, pursuing diversions "as if they could annihilate eternity by keeping their minds off of it."[9]

Ironically, the quest for immediate happiness typically distracts the one seeking it from the reality of the present moment, a painful and empty reality that only God can transform. "We never keep to the present," Pascal insisted, and so "we never actually live, but hope to live, and since we are always planning how to be happy, it is inevitable that we should never be so."[10] In a manner that resonates with certain Buddhist prescriptions, Pascal advocated cultivating a mindfulness of the present, resisting distractions even when they take the form of attractive promises. The mindful individual (according to Buddhism as well as on Pascal's account) will contemplate the emptiness of human existence, not as some morbid preoccupation, but as a spiritually edifying discipline.

This connection between boredom and religious edification is one that Kierkegaard was also careful to observe (an observation, however, that he sometimes communicated "indirectly"). Nowhere is he more eloquent in addressing the topic of boredom than when he speaks through the pseudonymous voice of "A" in the first volume of *Either/Or.* "A" contends: "Boredom is the root of all evil." He regards it as peculiar that boredom, "in itself so staid and solid, should have such power to set in motion. The influence that it exerts is altogether magical, except that it is not the influence of attraction, but of repulsion."[11]

Since Kierkegaard's "A" is the paradigmatic aesthete, his dramatically negative portrayal of boredom should be understood neither in religious nor in ethical terms. Indeed, the "evil" being contemplated here is more akin to bad art than to moral wickedness. In their desire to flee boredom and pursue the interesting, "A" observes, persons can frequently behave in the most boring and unimaginative ways.

> The gods were bored, and so they created man. Adam was bored because he was alone, and so Eve was created. Thus boredom entered the world, and increased in proportion to the increase in population. Adam was bored alone; then Adam and Eve were bored together; then Adam and Eve and Cain and Abel were bored *en famille;* then the population of the world increased, and the peoples were bored *en masse.* To divert themselves they conceived the idea of constructing a tower high enough to reach the heavens. This idea is itself as boring as the tower was high, and constitutes a terrible proof of how boredom gained the upper hand.[12]

Here the Tower of Babel is the symbolic precursor of all types of diversion, but of artistic creations in particular. Clearly, boredom is the great enemy of the aesthete and it is from the negative power of boredom that the aesthetic impulse draws much of its vitality. Kierkegaard's subject matter in these pages, however, is a somewhat restricted notion of the aesthetic. Nor does the aesthete's evaluation of boredom closely correspond to Kierkegaard's own. "A" is concerned with precisely how one ought to act in response to boredom's "power to set in motion." His goal is constantly to elude boredom, to be engaged in the perpetual cultivation of interest. Kierkegaard, like Pascal, displayed a somewhat ambivalent attitude toward boredom. While being bored is not in itself a praiseworthy condition, neither is it a laudable strategy to organize one's behavior around the avoidance of it. Moreover, no action or behavior ought to be recommended simply because it is interesting.

I want to observe that the relationship between boredom and the creative imagination is an exceedingly complex one. It is true that an artwork is generally considered to be a failure if it is boring.[13] Moreover, art is valued, in no small measure, because it elicits and sustains imaginative play; in doing so, it amuses or interests us, relieves us of our boredom. Providing such relief, in some instances, may be the primary motivation for the aesthetic; here, the creation and enjoyment of art can be characterized as strategies of diversion. But since the imagination can be employed for a variety of purposes other than pure entertainment, this characterization is not in all cases an inevitable one. As Kierkegaard himself recognized, art has a certain edifying power, the potential to unmask as well as to conceal both the source of boredom and its peculiar effects.

In what, more precisely, does the repulsive power of boredom consist? "A," overwhelmed by a "terrible tedium," reports in one of the moody meditations from his "Diapsalmata" that "the only thing I see is emptiness, the only thing I move about in is emptiness."[14] Compare this depiction of boredom with Pascal's: "Boredom depends on the nothingness which pervades reality; it causes a dizziness like that produced by looking down into a yawning chasm, and this dizziness is infinite. The eccentric form of diversion . . . sounds forth without producing an echo, which proves it to be based on boredom; for in nothingness not even an echo can be produced."[15] In its "eccentric form," diversion is "misdirected" and "conceals boredom within its own depths." Such diversion is most frequently manifested as a "restless activity that excludes a man from the world of the spirit." The person who appears busiest is likely to be the one most bored. Indeed, the "busiest workers . . . are the most tiresome of creatures." An "industrious zeal," generated in the vain hope of defeating a profound tedium, is typically its chief symptom. Work is the opposite of idleness, but no amount of work can annul boredom.

The aesthete's criticism of certain strategies of diversion is grounded solely in an evaluation of their ineffectiveness; the goal of diversion, the devotion to the "interesting," are themselves admirable. While "A" will recommend the "rotation method" as a more promising strategy for combating boredom, it is dubious that such a method itself evades the charge of "eccentricity." Here the pursuit of diversion seems to have been pushed to its logical extreme. In order to avoid boredom, the aesthete even "poetizes" existence, transforming the actual objects of sense perception into the perfected, idealized objects of the imagination, that is, into pure possibilities.[16] Once "de-actualized," the world of the aesthete can be imaginatively transfigured at will; it becomes an endless source of novelty and amusement. Nevertheless, the price of this pleasure is extraordinarily high: the aesthete gains a vast treasure house of potential diversions, only to lose the actual world.

It is important to note how the aesthete achieves this "poetizing" effect, by means of creative remembering and forgetting. Here the accent is on forgetfulness, since "remembering poetically is just another expression for forgetting," a transformation of experience by means of which it loses "all its painful aspects."[17] Even a pleasant experience, once past, ought to be forgotten, precisely because it has "as past something unpleasant about it, by which it stirs a sense of privation." Consequently, the rotation method is an attempt to defeat time by ignoring its reality, suppressing its effects, much as a drug might be used by a less creative individual. This is a highly artful form of self-deception, different from the sort of diversionary tactics described by Pascal and Thoreau only to the extent that it presupposes an extraordinarily fertile imagination. Such ingenuity merely masks the profound unhappiness of one who, fearing the emptiness of life even more than death, "is always absent, never present to himself."[18]

Unhappiness, even an unhappiness bordering on despair, is not a state of mind to be avoided at all cost. When unhappiness takes the form of an overpowering boredom, a terrifying meaninglessness, the great temptation will be to flee from this condition, taking refuge in some diversion. Moreover, on Kierkegaard's account, virtually any human action taken in response to boredom can become a diversionary tactic. While the desert fathers recommended manual labor as a potential remedy for the ennui that can plague the spiritual life, Kierkegaard seemed dubious about the possibility that work is a reliable cure for boredom. The most energetic form of labor, if it is conceived as a means for overcoming boredom, as a recipe for happiness, will very likely conceal boredom "within its depths." It may suffice to relieve boredom in its simpler forms, but it cannot eradicate the dizzying emptiness that Kierkegaard discovered at the source of "tedium" in its more terrifying manifestations. No humanly conceived prescription can cure the "sickness unto death."

"The possibility of this sickness is man's advantage over the beast," Kierkegaard wrote, "and it is an advantage that characterizes him quite otherwise than the upright posture, for it bespeaks the infinite erectness or loftiness of his being spirit. The possibility of this sickness is man's advantage over the beast; to be aware of this sickness is the Christian's advantage over natural man; to be cured of this sickness is the Christian's blessedness."[19] Boredom is a malaise that afflicts a self that has become problematic to itself. The individual who flees boredom through diversion is in a doubly problematic condition, even further removed "from the truth and deliverance."[20] Such a person is the victim of a "despair which is ignorant of being despair";[21] his is truly "a feeling of nullity without realizing it." On Kierkegaard's account, it is the Christian's "advantage" to be aware of his spiritual condition. One can conceive of this advantage in semiotic terms. The crucial difference between a boredom of which I am aware and one that lies "concealed within the depths" of my ongoing activity is the fact that only the former is accessible, available to be interpreted as a sign, and so potentially meaningful.

The project of exposing "concealed" boredom and of discerning its true nature is one to which Heidegger devoted considerable attention. Heidegger joined Pascal and Kierkegaard in believing boredom to have a profound metaphysical, if not explicitly religious, significance. In those various ways in which we contrive to "pass the time" we manage to "shake off" our boredom, causing it to "fall asleep." The most serious effort must therefore be devoted to "awakening" boredom, in the process of doing so, to recognizing its status as a fundamental human "attunement."[22]

Now for Heidegger attunements are "not merely subjectively coloured experiences or epiphenomenal manifestations of psychological life," but rather, they are to be conceived as fundamental ways of being, as "ways of *Dasein* in which *Dasein* becomes manifest to itself."[23] Consequently, boredom is not something we ought to resist; rather, we must find a way to "make room" for our boredom, to allow it to "resonate." Nevertheless, our typical response is to oppose it, to drive it away, so that boredom "will originally manifest itself . . . *wherever* we create a diversion from boredom for ourselves, where we in each case *pass the time* in such and such a way and with this intent."[24]

In its simplest form, we experience boredom as a being "bored by" something or other. We are "held fast" by a specific object or situation, but not in a way that the object is able to engage our interest; rather we are "left empty": "We are interested neither in the object nor in the result of the activity, but in *being occupied as such* and in this alone. We are seeking to be occupied in any way. Why? Merely so as not to fall into this *being left empty* that is emerging in boredom."[25]

Even in this simple form, boredom is already perceived as being rooted in an experience of emptiness, the emptiness of each passing moment, as well as of the object that confronts us and of the situation that binds us. The feeling of constraint is overpowering in these simple cases, a feeling that "in boredom we are *bound* precisely by—nothing."[26] We are not bound by time but by the emptiness of *this* time, and boredom is possible at all, in Heidegger's view, only because every object has its special time. And so we find ourselves in the condition of passing the time, killing this time, not at all directed toward time, but looking for something to divert our attention from it, to occupy us. If we successfully divert our attention, then, "in a certain way we forget time altogether."[27] For Heidegger, too, our diversions are exercises in forgetfulness.

At a deeper level, we are no longer "bored by" a particular object or activity, but rather we *ourselves* are bored. In this more profound state of boredom we experience a certain detachment from the objects that immediately confront us, so that our boredom begins to "radiate out" over other things.[28] Here is the recognition of a form of boredom that I have described as dispositional, not confined to precise circumstances or clearly limited in duration, but vague and lingering.

It is this indeterminate character of the second form of boredom, a certain quality of detachment, I will want to suggest, that helps to account for its potentially religious significance. There is no determinate being here that we can identify as "boring." This form of boredom is also more intensely self-reflexive than the first. While my boredom is always something that I myself must experience, in this deeper form it is more directly about my own being (*Dasein*) than some other being. Time does not seem to drag so terribly in this state, but we do experience a casual "abandoning of ourselves to whatever is going on," a "slipping away from ourselves."[29] We take time in order to "spend" it; the time slips away and leaves us empty.

Deeper still, in its third and most profound form, is a boredom that Heidegger described in quasi-mystical language. In such a state of being, I am neither bored with some particular thing nor is it correct to say that I myself am bored. Rather, "it is boring for one. It— for one—not for me as me, not for you as you, not for us as us, but *for one*. Name, standing, role, age and fate as mine and yours disappear. To put it more clearly, precisely this 'it is boring for one' makes all things disappear."[30]

Here, yet again, is the experience of a great emptiness, but not one that arises out of particular circumstances. Indeed, to be bored in this way is to want or expect nothing from the various beings that one encounters in given situations. This boredom has the effect of making "everything of equally great and equally little worth." All and everything appears indifferent to us. The emptiness consists precisely in the fact of this "*indifference* enveloping beings *as a whole*."[31] These beings do not disappear, but rather, they themselves appear as empty in the shadowy light of this pervasive and powerful indifference.

Such indifference is a vehicle of transcendence for Heidegger, "elevating" the bored person beyond specific circumstances and particular beings. One feels removed from the flow of time, experiences a kind of timelessness, as the beings that fill up time "recede into indifference."[32] Consequently, it would be useless to attempt to suppress this boredom, by passing the time, or spending time with some diversion. Moreover, "this boredom wishes to tell us something" and compels us to listen.[33] In the fundamental attunement of boredom, for those who are awakened by it and to it, the whole of being is revealed.

> Precisely when we are not absorbed in things or in our own selves, this "wholeness" comes over us—for example, in real boredom. Real boredom is still far off when this book

57

or that play, this activity or that stretch of idleness merely bores us. Real boredom comes when "one is bored." This profound boredom, drifting hither and thither in the abysses of existence like a mute fog, draws all things, all men and oneself along with them, together in a queer kind of indifference. This boredom reveals what-is in totality.

There is another possibility of such revelation, and that is in the joy we feel in the presence of the being—not merely the person—of someone we love.[34]

Already in its earlier manifestations, but especially in this third form, the experience of boredom is potentially revelatory, much like the experience of great love. In contrast to a trivial tedium or a superficial affection, both profound boredom and true love reveal the very depths of being itself. Being bored like this, loving like this, both presuppose a certain detachment from our normal way of experiencing the world. In each there is the dawning of an awareness of the presence of being in its wholeness, an awareness typically dimmed by our ongoing, everyday encounter with things.

Now since I have already characterized boredom, at least in some instances, as a failure to love, this analogy of Heidegger's may seem a bit puzzling at first blush (an appearance undoubtedly nourished by the immediate oddness of the analogy itself). Yet that earlier characterization was of a kind of boredom that can be portrayed as resembling acedia; that is, a boredom that I can be held responsible for, either in its genesis or its persistence. One of the distinguishing marks of acedia is that the bored person does not care much about being bored in this way. Such boredom can represent a refusal to love, to pay attention in a manner that love requires,

58

whereas a patient love that endures boredom can grow deeper and stronger.

For Heidegger, quite clearly, my boredom is a fact to which I should pay careful attention, a fundamental attunement that must be "awakened." This boredom is good for something, revealing the "whole of being," exposing *Dasein* in all of its finitude. Immersed in "everydayness," it is easy for us to ignore the specific way of being that is "essential" to the things around us. We experience each of them as "simply something present at hand in the broadest sense."[35] This way of experiencing the world is normal, comfortable, secure. While not to be "disparaged as something purely negative," nevertheless, our ordinary understanding of things is a kind of forgetfulness, most importantly, a forgetfulness of ourselves. In contrast, profound boredom can result in our "being drawn into a moment of vision," a moment in which "the utter abyss of *Dasein*" is disclosed.[36]

This is a moment, Heidegger insisted, that philosophy can only prepare us for, can never actually bring about. Indeed, our awakening to this vision is not a consequence either of skill or proper motivation. Rather, it "falls due to us only if we have waited for it and are able to wait." Moreover, (and here Heidegger's remarks take on some of the characteristics of religious discourse) "only whoever honors a mystery gains the strength to wait."[37] Like Ignatius, as with Zen Buddhism, so too with Heidegger, this transforming insight is always, in certain important respects, gratuitous. (Here the metaphor of "awakening" is employed felicitously, since being awakened from a slumber is more definitively something that happens to me than it is anything that I actively bring about.)[38]

Whatever else it may disclose, this "moment of vision" is about death, the radical finitude of *Dasein*, of my being as a being toward death. On Heidegger's account, "it is precisely death that illuminates the essence of life." Consciousness of death reveals the emptiness of beings. This dying to the world of beings, this loss of a world that we seem to possess so securely in our everydayness, reduces us to a "poverty" from which nevertheless "we can draw our own peculiar power of procuring transparency and inner freedom for *Dasein*."[39] Echoing Saint Paul, Heidegger described such poverty as a "kind of having in which we seem not to have." Here the echoes of Pascal and Kierkegaard also clearly reverberate. Boredom is an experience of having plenty of nothing. But this "nothing" matters.

THE CONNECTION between boredom and death has been already firmly established, albeit vaguely described. Boredom itself represents the death of meaning, of interest. It is an experience (however dimly understood as such) of the emptiness that lurks at the heart of human existence, an emptiness into which each moment fades, into which all finite things pass away. From a variety of perspectives, then, boredom is "about" death; yet it is a curious fact that death itself is not boring, that the mere awareness of death serves frequently enough to restore meaning and flavor to life. The recognition of approaching death might drain any particular human project or goal of its meaning, making it appear trivial, suddenly insignificant. But the threat of death usually suffices to render life *itself* precious—that is, life *as a whole.*

For example, consider a classroom filled with bored students as the lecturer drones on interminably. The sudden occurrence of a violent earthquake or the appearance of a maniacal terrorist firing rounds of live ammunition just over the heads of the students would undoubtedly cure their tedium. They would no longer be bored, yet it would be wrong to say that they had suddenly become interested in that particular lecture or in its subject matter. Rather, they themselves would no longer be bored.

The gift of potential meaning that death signifies is one that it requires a certain amount of courage and (I will propose) indifference in order clearly to discern.[40] In a situation of extreme crisis, when the overpowering reality of death is thrust upon us, perceptions and values may be dramatically transformed in an instant (like Saint Paul's own sudden conversion while en route to Damascus). More commonly, death lurks in the background, remains implicit and only vaguely recognized, creeping into our lives rather than taking us by storm. On those various occasions in which persons feel "bored to death," it is difficult for them to resist finding ways to "kill the time." Whether or not, on any given occasion, succumbing to this temptation constitutes a serious failure is always, as I have tried to suggest, a matter of interpretation.

The connection between boredom and attention has

also already been observed. And here, too, there are some curious facts worth considering. Boredom is often blamed for a failure to pay attention. Yet boredom itself, at least on some accounts and in some instances, is a significant phenomenon that merits attention. Indeed, the rabid pursuit of diversion has been criticized so harshly by Pascal and others precisely because they interpreted it as a dangerous refusal to pay attention to one's own experience of boredom.

As I will use the word, "distraction" represents the failure to pay attention to some specific object of concern (such as a person, a text, a concept, or an activity). Bored persons are easily distracted. I want to distinguish, however, between a diversion as that which I pursue when bored and a distraction as that which pursues me. The former is something that I seek, the latter, something to which I succumb. Moreover, diversions are attempts to fill up empty time, responses to boredom that do not always involve an explicit recognition of being in this condition. In such a state of emptiness, I may not be attending to anything in particular— instead, may be searching desperately for something to engage me. On the other hand, distraction occurs in situations that are more determinate, in cases where I am trying (or ought to be trying) to concentrate on this particular X, but my attention keeps slipping away, fastening upon other objects of interest.

"Distraction" sounds like something negative, but this too is open to interpretation. If my studies or my meditation are interrupted by the noise from a television set in the next room or if I am distracted from my beloved's presence by extraneous thoughts about tomorrow afternoon's business agenda, then I might regard my condition as problematic. But if my attention to X is disturbed by my child's hysterical sobbing or by someone's sudden cry for help or by a stunningly beautiful sunset, then it may seem necessary to evaluate the situation differently. It may be deemed appropriate in such cases, even obligatory, to attend to my distractions.

Meaning is a semiotic event. Different persons interpret the meaning of specific things and situations differently. And so it stands to reason that one person's object of attention will be another person's distraction. It also makes sense to propose that, over time, any given individual's attention will shift, so that what once preoccupied me as important might now be regarded as a disturbing nuisance. The act of paying attention is by its very nature a highly selective phenomenon. Choosing what to pay attention to, especially for persons living in a "high information" society, is an extraordinarily complex interpretative judgment. Boredom challenges the choices that we make, introducing the threat of distraction. In an environment where the array of choices is staggeringly wide, the potential for cognitive and emotional "numbness" is frighteningly real. This also is a species of boredom, the deeper form of meaninglessness that Pascal, Kierkegaard, and Heidegger all struggled to expose.

The possibility of "good distractions" notwithstanding, my earlier portrayal of acedia indicates that distraction can be a serious problem from a religious point of view, eroding religious commitment and effectively undermining spiritual practices. Often, the problem is regarded as being symptomatic of a certain weakness of will on the part of the person distracted. This is quite typical of talk about acedia. Here the object of attention (the divine good) is judged to be, in itself, of infinite interest. Consequently, the experience of boredom and vulnerability to distraction are facts that require some explanation. Among a variety of plausible candidates is a failure to fasten the grip of attention securely enough on its object; distractions arise, this grip is easily broken, and attention slips away.

Where the primary problem is a weakness of will, exercises designed to strengthen volition represent an important strategy for coping with distractions. Recall the lively images of a "spiritual combat," prominent within the history of Christian spirituality. Distractions that arise to disrupt spiritual practices do not occur in a merely serendipitous fashion; they are the work of an enemy who preys especially on the weak (and here boredom is an important sign of weakness).

In order to resist such an enemy, Cassian argued, the devotee should work tirelessly to cultivate *fortitudo,* since the virtues of fortitude and patience are most directly opposed to acedia as a vice. At first inspection, this account may seem to conflict with Aquinas's later analysis of acedia as being in opposition to caritas; more specifically, it is a sorrowfulness signifying the lack of joy that such a love engenders. But the appearance of any important disagreement here is misleading, since Aquinas also clearly perceived patience (a species of fortitude) as the offspring of caritas, citing no lesser authority than Saint Paul on this issue.⁴¹ Moreover, Aquinas was emphatic, as I have already observed, in advocating a vigorous resistance to the onslaught of acedia, prescribing, as the best antidote for troubling distractions, a willful perseverance.

"To persevere in patience" is also the counsel that Ignatius supplied in his *Exercises* for the victims of desolation. In such a state, the individual is vulnerable to every form of distraction: mental agitation, emotional vexation, temptation. Consequently, it becomes especially important not only to stay the course, but actually to redouble one's efforts in meditation: "We must remember that during the time of consolation it is easy, and requires only a slight effort, to continue a whole hour in contemplation, but in time of desolation it is very difficult to do so. Hence, in order to fight against the desolation and conquer the temptation, the exercitant must always remain in the exercise a little more than the full hour. Thus he will accustom himself not only to resist the enemy, but even to overthrow him."⁴²

Even so gentle a spirit as Saint Francis de Sales was inclined to employ the same type of martial imagery and to give very much the same sort of advice. When you experience a boredom so overpowering that you find yourself doing everything "coldly, sadly and sluggishly," nevertheless, he admonished, "you must persevere," precisely because it is by means of sorrow that "the enemy tries to make us weary of good works."⁴³

The body of advice supplied by the Christian literature on the problem of distraction is by no means as

65

homogeneous as these few examples might tend to suggest. But the diversity of perspectives on this issue is best displayed by extending one's purview beyond Christianity. For example, the Hasidim recommended a strategy for coping with distractions in prayer that differs dramatically from this policy of resistance. Rather than oppose distracting images or ideas, seeking by an act of will to expel them from consciousness, the devotee is encouraged actively to pursue and embrace such thoughts!

> Even the distracting thoughts that confound you during prayer may be a good sign. . . .
> . . . When a distracting thought comes to you in prayer, hold fast to God and break through to redeem the sacred spark that dwells within that thought.[44]

For the Ba'al Shem Tov and his followers, the distractions that frequently accompany boredom can possess a religious significance. The key to perceiving them as such, to recognizing them as signs and interpreting their meaning, is a cultivated indifference. Once detached both from self and from the material world, the devotee discovers that "there can be no distractions. Nothing can disturb such prayer."[45] A pious indifference removes all obstacles between the one who prays and the object of devotion by transforming distractions into signs of the divine presence and purpose. Outside of the God to whom one prays, "nothing" exists. That is to say, apart from God, all things are nothing but distractions. To the person who is properly disposed, however, this nothing matters; it becomes a sign radiantly charged with sacred meaning.

The difference noted here between Christian and Jewish teachings about distraction in prayer is one of emphasis and approach, rather than a fundamental contrast in principle. In the first place, the Hasidic masters certainly did not fail to regard the spiritual life as involving a kind of spiritual warfare, recommending, for example, that morning prayer should always begin before dawn, when "one can still combat the destructive forces of the coming day."[46] More importantly, even Ignatius was careful to admit (as I have already observed) that the "enemy" may not be responsible for every case of desolation and distraction; God may permit or cause them to occur for specific reasons that the devotee must be able to discern. On Ignatius's account, as with Hasidism, it is an attitude of indifference that best disposes a person to recognize the will of God. From both perspectives, then, spiritual boredom and its concomitant distractions can be religiously meaningful signs.

Consider, as a final example, the teachings of Zen Buddhism on the topic of distraction in meditation. The pragmatic core of this teaching consists in the recommendation that one ought neither to resist nor to pursue extraneous thoughts that arise during the practice of zazen. In order that they might cause the least amount of disturbance to the mind, one is encouraged simply to remain "still" and to observe these distractions as they enter and eventually exit consciousness.

"When you are practicing zazen, do not try to stop your thinking. Let it stop by itself. If something comes into your mind, let it come in, and let it go out. It will not stay long. When you try to stop your thinking, it means you are bothered by it. Do not be bothered by anything."[47] From a Buddhist perspective that advocates the transcendence of ordinary cognition as a religious ideal, all thoughts and images are potential distractions. Yet the possibility that such distractions might represent the work of an "enemy" is rejected, implicitly in the quotation above, explicitly by the Vietnamese Zen master Thich Nhat Hanh. He gently warns his readers of the temptation to perceive "unwholesome thoughts" as

> an enemy force which is trying to disturb the concentration and understanding of your mind. But, in fact, when we are angry, *we ourselves* are anger. . . . When we have certain thoughts, *we are those thoughts.* . . .
> . . . Therefore, chasing away or dwelling on any thought isn't the important thing. The important thing is to be aware of the thought.[48]

This counsel contrasts with the Christian teaching about distraction; it is equally far removed from the Hasidic instruction on this topic. Indeed, I want to insist that there are important differences among all of these traditions of spirituality, as well as a rich diversity of perspectives within each. Nevertheless, my present interest attaches more to the continuities than to the differences among them. Of course, exposing these continuities among perspectives is a very different matter from arguing that they are essentially the "same."

Any given thing will be like any other thing, at least in some respect. To observe this likeness is to discover a continuity between them; but it is not to conclude that they are "the same thing."

The historical relationship between Zen and certain Asian martial traditions is too well established for it to be supposed that the Buddhists have eschewed all talk of a spiritual combat. Thich Nhat Hanh's warning is best construed as a plea for the recognition that this combat is not one in which I violently engage some "other." If there is an "enemy" here, it is none other than the self, more determinately, the "narrow" self that is confounded by ignorance, an ego blinded by its own desires and attachments. Consequently, it is a practiced indifference that will supply the key to victory in this contest. It also supplies the thread of continuity that I am struggling to expose.

For the Zen Buddhist, to be genuinely mindful is to be occupied with no particular thought or mental image. Paradoxically, mindfulness is embodied most perfectly in a consciousness that is "empty" and detached. Attending to no specific thing, such a mind is able effectively to attend to anything, without prejudice or illusion. The logic supporting such a claim deserves careful inspection. But first I want to consider briefly one of the primary Zen strategies for achieving a state of mindfulness and defeating distractions. It is the use of breath and breathing to focus attention and cultivate detachment. A peaceful mind is maintained in this fashion, while a scattered mind is recollected and restored.

The breath is a "bridge" that provides a vital link

between body and mind, between the inner world and the outer world.[49] The meditative discipline of paying attention to breathing is itself a bridge that links Zen Buddhism to the ancient wisdom embodied in the Yoga Sutras and classical Taoism. In Hasidism, pure prayer is identified with "holy breath"; the one who prays is likened to a "ram's horn," in itself empty, but precisely as such, a powerful instrument through and from which the divine word can sound forth.[50] Ignatius of Loyola's "third method of prayer" involves the use of the breath to regulate attention in the recitation of specific vocal prayers.[51] In all of these cases, my interest is not so much in the specific methods of meditation employed as in the principle that informs them.

Zen Buddhists have articulated this principle with a singular clarity. In the relaxed, continuous practice of attentive breathing, the mind is empty, focused on nothing apart from the breath, yet aware of everything that is present. "Nothingness is always there, and from it everything appears."[52] And so this mindful state is one of emptiness, but also of readiness for whatever might appear. The steady, repetitive flow of breathing calms the mind, renders it soft and supple like the breath itself. A mind thus disposed yields to distractions without surrendering to them; rather, their own emptiness is exposed, robbing them of any power that they might otherwise have over the mind. This practice requires persistence, a constancy, the ability to wait patiently but with no determinate set of expectations.

Contrast the peaceful, steady breathing of a mindful person with the heavy sighing of someone dreadfully bored. Here breathing itself is a sign, a behavioral cue that signals to the observer different states of heart and mind. By what additional criteria does one distinguish the calm detachment of the one from the numbing indifference of the other? How might the latter be transformed into a loving attentiveness, no less detached? And by what measures can the former be safeguarded from the danger of slipping into a drowsy or distracted state, or even worse, from plunging into ennui's darkest abyss?

3

NOTHING
MATTERS

The Logic of Indifference

Indifference, disinterestedness, detachment. Like boredom itself, these are ambiguous concepts, since my lack of care or interest, my disengagement, can be viewed in either a positive or a negative light. The experience of boredom seems more closely related to these phenomena in their negative manifestations (so that the calm, detached, meditative consciousness is not typically portrayed as one that is "bored"). But there is no simple rule governing the usage of these terms, since persons will often judge objects or situations to be of such little value that the wise individual will tend to be bored by them, only the foolish or vulgar person regarding them with interest.

The judgment that something is unworthy of my interest does not result automatically in an appropriate feeling of boredom. Disinterest, like interest, often needs to be cultivated, even practiced. In contrast, a person may be victimized by feelings of boredom that arise uninvited and unwanted. Here a person has a sense of being trapped by such feelings—suffocated and oppressed. This contrast is relevant to my axiological considerations. "Good" boredom is the sort of thing that one would tend to cultivate. "Bad" boredom represents a failure, or afflicts like a disease.

The connection between willing and feeling is by no means so simple that the latter can be regarded as a sign yielding consistently accurate information about the nature of one's intentions. If I could always manage to feel exactly how I want and ought to feel, then the experience of boredom would never produce anxiety. As William James pointed out, meaning is often experienced as something "given," whatever role that one might play in its discovery. At the same time, James seemed clearly to argue that we are partially responsible for the quality of our experiences, for helping to make them meaningful, and that this is all a matter of exercising our volitional musculature.[1]

I construe the judgment that "one ought to care about X" primarily as a judgment not about how one ought to feel, but rather about the quality of one's attention. Boredom can defeat attention; but I can succeed in paying attention despite my boredom, and sometimes even generate interest as a consequence of doing so. Attention is subject to my control in a way that boredom is not. This sort of self-control will have some effect on the way that I feel, perhaps not directly or immediately, but in a gradual way, through the development of tendencies or habits of feeling.

If the connection between boredom and volition were less complex, then it would be possible to delineate the ethics of ennui in a relatively straightforward manner. Willing would be related to feeling as cause to effect. Specific feelings could be interpreted as signs revealing indexically the operation of certain corresponding volitions. Appropriate judgments could readily be formulated, responsibility easily imputed, given the obvious simplicity of this causal connection.

Not only is this causal connection far from simple, moreover, feelings can represent the starting point rather than the upshot of some morally significant endeavor. As I have tried to suggest, the theological literature about boredom displays less concern with how one came to feel bored than with what one proceeds to do in response to the feeling. What one decides to do itself presupposes an ability to discern the meaning of one's experience. My sense that "nothing matters" can take the form either of a boredom close to despair or of a religious insight, powerful and liberating. So this business of discernment is hardly a trivial matter.

The importance of discernment is underscored by Ignatius of Loyola in his *Spiritual Exercises*, the primary goal of which is to facilitate a process of decision making. As a general principle, one ought to decide to conform oneself entirely to the will of God. Yet, like all important decisions, this one needs to be carefully informed. To do the will of God requires first that one be able, in various situations and on different occasions, to *know* the will of God. This latter is the task of discernment.

Embodied within the "First Principle and Foundation" of the *Exercises* is the Ignatian prescription that "we must make ourselves indifferent to all created things."[2] The concept of indifference receives a somewhat more elaborate treatment at a later point in the text, as part of a broader consideration of the appropriate methods for spiritual decision making. Here, Ignatius advises,

> It is necessary to keep as my aim the end for which I am created, that is, the praise of God our Lord and the salvation of my soul. Besides this, I must be indifferent, without any inordinate attachment, so that I am not more inclined or disposed to accept the object in question than to relinquish it, nor to give it up than to accept it. I should be like a balance at equilibrium, without leaning to either side, that I might be ready to follow whatever I perceive is for the glory and praise of God our Lord and for the salvation of my soul.[3]

Ignatian indifference is a matter of how one is disposed and, at the same time, a neutralizing of those dispositions that typically give shape to our desires and preferences—what Ignatius here calls "inclinations." Indifference is itself a habitual state—describable, somewhat paradoxically, as a disposition not to be disposed, and more straightforwardly and positively, as a state of *readiness*, a disposition to respond, under any circumstances, to the divine will. The Jesuit theologian Karl Rahner explained that the achievement of this state requires first the detachment of oneself "from every determinate thing" that one might be tempted to regard as the precise locus of divine revelation. For exactly this reason, "*indiferencia* becomes a seeking of God in all things," a readiness to meet God anywhere.[4] Moreover, "this finding of God in everything . . . is only the persistent putting into practice of a supernatural concrete logic, of discovering the will of God through the experimental test of consolation."[5]

Two observations concerning Rahner's explanation can be brought to bear on the topic under consideration. The first concerns his insistence that the "concrete logic" of the *Exercises* is something other than a form of deductive logic.[6] The second observation, one of more immediate concern, attaches to his remarks about the "experimental test of consolation." (Underlying both observations is the insight linking indifference to indeterminacy.)

Advice about spiritual consolation and desolation forms the substance of Ignatius's "Rules for the Discernment of Spirits," which appear toward the end of the *Spiritual Exercises*. These rules identify consolation as an "interior joy" arousing the soul to a greater love of God. Desolation has already been described here as the opposite condition, a "darkness of soul" in which all joy is extinguished. Recall that both consolation and desolation were regarded by Ignatius as signs, the proper interpretation of which is governed by the logic of indifference. This logic suggests that one ought to detach oneself from "every determinate thing" or practice that one might be tempted to regard as embodying the promise of consolation. Thus detached, one may come to perceive desolation itself as a powerful sign both of human finitude and of the divine transcendence. Interpreted as such, these feelings signify the fact that religious insight is neither produced nor controlled through simple acts of volition. It bears the character of a gift, the fruits of which may linger for a time but cannot be preserved indefinitely. Even in the absence of genuine consolation, desolation can function as a sign of the gratuitous quality of this "interior joy"; as such, it is an absence that reveals the presence of a divine giver, a gracious God.

Nevertheless, it is important to remember that not every experience of desolation is to be interpreted in this fashion. To assume otherwise would be to violate the logical principle just established by attempting to transform desolation itself into a determinate locus of divine revelation—ironically, to take consolation in one's desolation. But this acute form of spiritual boredom may signal instead one's own sinful laxity in devotion, or it may be perceived as a test of one's spiritual mettle. In each case, recall that Ignatius encouraged the exercitant to persist in his meditations, in continuous readiness, with patient endurance.

The "Rules for the Discernment of Spirits" incorporates Ignatius's description of a consolation that is "without previous cause."[7] Unlike consolations that are conjoined to a particular practice or result from the contemplation of some definite spiritual good, this type is "without any preceding perception or knowledge of any subject by which a soul might be led to such consolation through its own acts of intellect and will." On Ignatius's account, God alone can give this consolation. Yet the individual can prepare for such an experience, once again, by cultivating an attitude of indifference, an openness or readiness to discern God's gracious will manifested in no particular thing and, thus, in any and every thing.

Such indifference constitutes one of the necessary conditions or rubrics for what Rahner identified as the "experimental test of consolation." This experiment is enacted, whenever particular things and situations are encountered with "pure openness and receptivity," in order that they might be interpreted properly as signs of God's will, God's grace. While feelings of desolation are among the data that require interpretation, I have suggested that they may also supply the appropriate conditions for Ignatius's "experiment," resulting in a similar detachment, a similar readiness. In any event, no religious insight is guaranteed by the simple fact of these conditions being in place. A proposition asserting the presence of such conditions would be linked to one affirming the expectation of insight by something considerably weaker than a relationship of entailment. This is not to deny the logical status of that relationship, but simply to observe that it lacks the necessary force of a logical deduction.

Ignatius is hardly unique in his observation of the spiritual fruits of detachment. Nor is he alone in his recognition that spiritual dryness or desolation can stimulate detachment and so produce good effects, comparable to those achieved in a state of more practiced indifference. From such a viewpoint, the experience of boredom can represent an important opportunity for spiritual exercise, even as it sometimes signals the failure to pursue such exercises with devotion. This contrast is not as sharp as it might initially appear, because, on Ignatius's account, my spiritual "failures" are also something that I need to become aware of, the fostering of such awareness itself representing one of the goals of spiritual discipline.

Consider John of the Cross's discussion of precisely this point. The dry, dark night of spiritual boredom has as its chief benefit, in his view, the causing of "knowledge of self and of one's own misery."[8] Clothed now in garments of "dryness" and "desolation," the soul "considers itself to be nothing . . . because it is aware that of itself it neither does nor can do anything." With "nothing to do," the individual suffers the risk of being overcome by boredom, driven by feelings of impotence to a state of anxiety, even despair. But John perceived this condition also as an invitation to stand firm, detached and watchful "in order to contemplate what God says to me."[9] Moreover, corresponding to this growth in self-awareness is a proportionate increase in knowledge of God. Once again, boredom is recognized as having a certain edifying power.

All of these remarks attach to what John understood as the first "dark night of the senses"—as such, potentially a species of "good boredom," to be distinguished from lukewarmness or slothfulness by the signs identified earlier. Nevertheless, while being careful to avoid any simple identification of spiritual dryness with acedia, I want to continue to insist that these categories of phenomena are necessarily fuzzy at the borders. Consider that the aridity produced by God in the soul for edifying purposes, on John's analysis, also has an important purgative function. This is true for the second "dark night of the spirit" as well, when even the serious devotee, advanced in contemplation, suffers a necessary affliction for the purpose of purgation; that is, because of habitual and actual imperfections in the soul that remain to be uprooted.[10] So while acedia may itself be a capital sin, the fact of human sinfulness is not altogether irrelevant to the experience of the "dark night," even when God is discerned to be the chief cause of these feelings of desolation and inappetence.

Perhaps the most vivid and moving image of a "holy indifference" produced by a Christian thinker is that presented by Saint Francis de Sales in his *Treatise on the Love of God*.[11] Like Ignatius and John, Francis insisted that such indifference must extend to all things, including, in the spiritual life, to experiences "such as dryness, consolation, relish, and aridity." The truly indifferent heart will love "tribulation as much as consolation, although the latter is more agreeable in itself." Indeed, for precisely this reason, it will have a "greater love for tribulation, because it sees in it nothing to be loved except the mark of God's will." Notice that Francis's argument here is semiotic in character. While consolation and desolation can both function as religiously meaningful signs, the latter has a greater potential effectiveness. Not attractive in itself or distracting attention to itself, it can serve more readily as the "mark" of God's will.

This discussion of indifference culminates in Francis's parable about "one of the world's finest musicians."[12] Having gradually become deaf, he can no longer take pleasure in the beauty of his music. And so he continues to sing and play only to please the prince in whose court he had been raised and to whom he owes an "infinite obligation." Sometimes, to "test" his musician's love, the prince instructs him to sing but then immediately leaves the room to pursue the hunt. Now, Francis observed of the musician, "he had neither pleasure in the melody, for his deafness deprived him of that, nor that of pleasing the prince, since the prince was absent and hence could not enjoy the sweetness of the beautiful airs that he sang." Yet the musician continues to sing as attentively and beautifully as if his lord were present in the room. This is Francis's image of a genuinely "holy indifference," one of the essential characteristics of the love of God. Individuals lacking such a quality of indifference run the risk of beginning to love God "for the pleasure they themselves take in the exercises of holy love. Instead of being in love with God, they fall in love with the love they have for him. They are attached to their own attachments. . . . They are content with this love because it is their own, because it is in their spirit and because it proceeds from them."[13]

In contrast, Francis evaluated as truly indifferent a love strong enough to endure being "unsupported by any pleasure or any expectation." Deprived of consolation, the soul "is sunk in spiritual anguish which renders love exceedingly pure and clean."[14] This is what John of the Cross described as the purgative effect of the soul's dark night. It is important to notice that, once immersed in this darkness, even love's divine object can become shrouded and disappear. In such a state, the soul wills nothing, directs its attention to no particular thing, plans nothing, aspires to nothing, takes pleasure in nothing.

> It seems to me that the soul that is in this state of indifference and wills nothing but leaves it to God to will what is pleasing to him must be said to have its will in a simple and general state of waiting. To wait is neither to do nor to act, but only to remain subject to some event. . . . It is not an action but rather a simple disposition to receive whatever shall happen.[15]

Indifference, disinterestedness, detachment. "Holy indifference" must be distinguished from a cold and empty indifference if it is to be understood as the quality of a perfect love. (Such a coldness in the musician's heart would surely infect the quality of his singing.) Disinterested here cannot mean uninterested. The latter signifies boredom as it is more commonly understood.[16] The former is a cultivated condition, a disposition, something practiced and achieved (that may, however, trace its roots to an original state of boredom as weary uninterest). In the religiously meaningful sense of this word, a "disinterested" person should be conceived as one who has "no determinate interest," rather than simply as one who has "no interest at all." To put it another way, disinterestedness may be described as involving not a *lack* of interests, but rather, a lively *play* of interests. (I will attempt to characterize the logic of

indifference as being in some sense "playful" below.)
Moreover, detachment is to be regarded as a species of
freedom, a refusal to be bound by one's own "attachments" or desires. In the teachings of the Bhagavad
Gita, human awareness is said to be clouded by desire.
By contrast, detachment is a spiritually lucid condition
transcending both passion and sloth, a peaceful state of
perfect equanimity.[17] In its religious usage, the concept
of detachment also frequently designates a mode of
readiness, a *waiting*, but not a waiting for anything in
particular.

This is the concept of detachment employed by
Meister Eckhart, when he admonished his readers to
"keep this in mind: to be full of things is to be empty
of God, while to be empty of things is to be full of
God."[18] Rather than a pure, blank nothing, such emptiness seems best construed as indeterminacy, a freedom
from the hegemony of "this or that." Here is an essential precondition (as with Ignatius) for knowing and
doing the will of God. "God is free to do his will on
his own level when my heart, being disinterested, is
bent on neither this or that."[19] Here also is a freedom
that brings peace, a freedom to "seek peace in all
things," and for Eckhart there is "no peace except in
disinterest."

Such disinterest is intended to defeat the spiritually
deadening effects of self-interest. "Think of yourself as
nothing," the Hasidic masters counseled, "and pray
only for the sake of God."[20] Throughout their deliberations, the quality of indifference is described as one
achieved through the continual embracing of nothing-

ness. Prayer begins, ideally, with a casting aside of limiting interests and attachments, an entering into "the endless world of Nothing." Eckhart's admonition echoes and reverberates in the teachings of the Hasidim. "Therefore, see yourself as nothing: only one who is nothing can contain the fullness of the Presence."[21]

This nothing matters precisely because of its potential to receive that "Presence." But the divine presence in itself is "no-thing"—that is, no determinate thing—so that the experience of absence, of nothingness, even of the emptiness of a lingering boredom, is more than simply a preparation for some later experience of fulfillment. As these spiritual writers delineate it, the logic of indifference stipulates a withdrawal from all determinacy, including specific concepts or images of the divine reality. The musician's song is purified and perfected in the absence of his prince, in an empty room. This emptiness is itself charged with religious meaning, not only for Jewish and Christian mystics, but emphatically so within Buddhism and Taoism as well.

Zen Buddhist talk about the emptiness of all things, their essential nothingness, is intended to assist the devotee in her achievement of a state of "no mind" *(mushin)*. But such a state is far removed from either a dreamy vacancy or a despairing meaninglessness. The Zen sage Takuan described it, rather, as an "unfettered" condition. The mind "neither congeals or fixes itself in one place" and "when this No-Mind has been well developed, the mind does not stop with one thing nor does it lack any one thing. It is like water overflowing and exists within itself. It appears appropriately when facing a time of need."[22]

The Zen practitioner, like the martial artist, is thus enabled, in "time of need," to respond to whatever challenges or threats might arise, either from without or from within. Here both the martial imagery and the symbolism of water have deep roots that can be traced back to origins in Chinese culture and to Taoism. The *Tao Te Ching* frequently employs water and its properties in order to exemplify *wu wei*, a disposition that manifests itself in a paradoxical mode of action, a doing without doing. By doing nothing, the Taoist sage teaches, everything is done: "Heaven does nothing to win the day; says nothing—is echoed; orders nothing—is obeyed; advises nothing—is right."[23]

Note again the peculiar potency of this concept of "nothing"—its strategic and spiritual significance. "Doing nothing" in this sense is not equivalent simply to refraining from doing anything. Rather, one does everything *as if* one were doing nothing, much as Saint Paul encouraged Christians to "have" all things as if they did not possess them. This was the concept of "poverty" that Heidegger invoked in his discussion of the most profound state of boredom. Trivial boredom is to be distinguished from a potentially revelatory indifference by the fact of its determinacy, its manifestation as a being bored with "this or that." In contrast, a profound boredom is dispositional and can manifest itself as a genuine "poverty of spirit," as something akin to the Buddhist state of *mushin*.[24]

From a semiotic perspective, then, "good" and "bad" boredom are not to be designated as perfectly discrete phenomena; they are best understood, as I have already suggested, in the terms supplied by a logic of vagueness, especially so when certain characteristics of the experience of boredom are left indeterminate with respect to differences in time. That is to say, one type of boredom can be transformed into another, depending upon how one proceeds to read the signs that constitute the fabric of human experience. From this perspective, the experience of great desolation can become a "mark" of the divine will, while even the most pious soul can become completely lost in the "dark night" and surrender to despair. On the accounts supplied by the spiritual writers from various traditions, this difference in outcome is a matter of discernment, but equally a matter of patience, humility, and courage. Finally, a genuinely positive outcome (the experience of insight, joyfulness) is not a result to be achieved, but rather, a state of affairs for which one must wait and (even in nontheistic traditions) for which one ought to feel grateful.

I WANT TO consider quite briefly and for purposes of comparison certain analyses of the aesthetic experience in which the concept of disinterestedness figures prominently. Some philosophers of art, much like the spiritual writers already surveyed, have prescribed an attitude of indifference as necessary in order to facilitate the experience of the beautiful. At the same time, the risk of boredom can represent a serious challenge to aesthetic experience, much as it threatens to overwhelm or undermine religious devotion. Once again, my attention is directed to the continuities among these otherwise disparate phenomena, to the threads of a common logic that they might share.

Consider first some isolated aspects of Kant's *Critique of Judgment*, especially part I of that treatise, dealing with judgments of taste. For Kant, the imagination and understanding are mutually related in any act of judgment; but in the aesthetic judgment there is no determinate concept that restricts these faculties to a specific rule of cognition. Consequently, "when such a judgment is pure, it connects liking or disliking directly with the mere *contemplation* of the object, irrespective of its use or any purpose."[25] Here the relationship of the faculties is characteristically free and playful, while aesthetic pleasure itself consists in the harmonious "free play" of the imagination and understanding.[26]

By contrast with logical judgments, in reflective judgments of taste no determinate concept is applied in advance to the thing under consideration. That is to say, in aesthetic contemplation, one does not evaluate a particular object simply by comparing it with the determinate, preformed class concept for things of that kind. Nevertheless, the imagination is still in harmony with the general requirements of the understanding. Every judgment that involves subsuming a given representation under a definite concept presupposes *a more general and indeterminate relationship* between the representation-producing faculty (imagination) and the concept-producing faculty (understanding). This general relationship is preserved even though the aesthetic

87

judgment does not connect an object with a specific concept of its nature or purpose.

It is not altogether clear to what extent Kant would want to say that concepts are at all involved in the aesthetic judgment. It seems plausible to me that they could be; that is, aesthetic judgments could involve a "playing with" the relationship between possible rules and representations, rather than being confined to or by a specific concept as in a logical judgment. Rooted in an openness, in a certain disinterested receptivity to the particular thing being contemplated, the aesthetic judgment might take the form of experimentation with a variety of concepts. This sort of cognitive play could involve the imaginative production of entirely new rules of thought or the reformulation of old rules shaped by actual encounter with the thing in question.

It is clear, however, that for Kant aesthetic pleasure does not result from subsuming some representation under a concept, but rather it is produced by the general harmony or free play of the faculties. It is in this respect, too, that the aesthetic judgment and the pleasure of the beautiful can be said to be "disinterested," in that every "interest" for Kant must involve the concept of what an object should be, as well as a concern with the actual existence of that object. "It seems, therefore, that only a lawfulness without a law, and a subjective harmony of the imagination with the understanding without an objective harmony—where the representation is referred to a determinate concept of an object—is compatible with the free lawfulness of the understanding (which has also been called purposiveness without a purpose) and with the peculiarity of a judgment of taste."[27]

The connection between these aesthetic deliberations and Kant's moral and religious doctrines is vague but important. The free play of imagination and understanding in the aesthetic judgment resembles, Kant suggested, the harmony of choice and reason in the moral judgment.[28] Furthermore, the disinterestedness of the aesthetic judgment finds a parallel in the (admittedly different kind of) disinterestedness that characterizes the moral judgment. Kant went so far as to propose that the experience of beauty might even prepare an individual to love something or someone disinterestedly, and thus that it has a potentially moral and religious significance. In any event, the logic of Kant's argument seems to me to have basic features in common with the Ignatian logic of indifference. Both the experience of beauty and the proper discernment of God's will presuppose a certain detachment from every determinate concept (whether it be the concept of some object or of some perceived spiritual good). This freedom from determinacy helps to make possible, without in itself causing, both the pleasure of the beautiful and the religious experience of consolation.

Against the background of these Kantian deliberations, Friedrich Schiller developed his own perspective on aesthetic experience as shaped by the play impulse (*Spieltrieb*). Within the playful consciousness, conflicting impulses are harmonized producing a "lofty equanimity and freedom of spirit."[29] This is a state of pure indifference, of pure "nullity," in which the self is disposed to no particular end or activity. It is a form of consciousness that is not predetermined while yet being genuinely open to determination. Consequently, this is a potentially fruitful nullity, undetermined but determinable, creative and free: "In the aesthetic state, man is Nought, if we are thinking of any particular result rather than of the totality of his powers, and considering the absence in him of any specific determination. Hence we must allow that those people are entirely right who declare beauty, and the mood it induces in us, to be completely indifferent . . .; for beauty produces no particular result whatsoever, neither for the understanding nor for the will. It accomplishes no particular purpose."[30]

Nothingness, indifference, indeterminacy, freedom. To the cluster of concepts already explored here in the consideration of various spiritual writers, Kant and Schiller now add the notion of playfulness. This is a notion that has its own peculiar religious history and significance, as a tracing of the etymological roots of both "play" and "contemplation" would suggest, and as the discussion of Peirce's "Musement" below will help to demonstrate.[31] But the immediate context for Schiller's treatment of the concept is a discussion of aesthetic sensibilities, even if one is forced already to observe in Schiller the lines of continuity that link his discourse on the beautiful to certain moral and religious concerns.

On Schiller's account, human behavior and experience are shaped by two conflicting impulses, one embracing change and sensuality (*Stofftrieb*), the other a rational drive toward ideal form and the eternal (*Formtrieb*). It is only within the context of the aesthetic experience that these contrary impulses are properly harmonized or balanced. Now recall the fact that this image of perfect "balance" is the one supplied by Ignatius of Loyola in his explication of the religious concept of indifference. For Schiller as well, disinterestedness consisted in the achievement of a certain psychic state of equilibrium. In such a state, the individual is an indeterminate "Nought," but in the special sense of being equipoised, open and free. If one were to employ the sort of talk that Taoists utilize in describing *wu wei*, this could be called an active passivity (or for Kant, a "purposiveness without a purpose"), not the mere absence of all dispositions but rather a cultivated disposition not to be inclined "here or there." It is aptly described as a state of readiness. Schiller makes the distinction clear at the beginning of his important "Twenty-First Letter": "The psyche may be said to be determinable simply because it is not determined at all; but it is also determinable inasmuch as it is determined in a way that does not exclude anything, i.e., when the determination it undergoes is of a kind which does not involve limitation. . . . the latter is aesthetic determinability (it has no limits, because it embraces all reality)."[32]

As in Pascal's meditations, Schiller's letters locate human beings midway between zero and infinity. The aesthetic consciousness is distinguished, however, precisely by the fact that it constitutes the realization of a state of nothingness that "embraces all reality." Free from the engagement of pursuing some finite end or interest, the playful mind is infinitely determinable. Neither immersed in a world of transient sense perceptions, nor fixed on some empty, abstract, eternal form, the disinterested player is "directed towards annulling time within time."[33]

Thus defined, the aesthetic experience supplies what the bored human psyche craves, a freedom from the burdens of time, the emptiness of time. Nevertheless, the "annulling" of time by the *Spieltrieb,* as Schiller portrayed it, is not to be understood as a recipe for "killing time," in the sense of a Pascalian diversion. Diversions take the form of a preoccupation with specific interests or objects of concern. The contemplation of beauty is characterized instead by its disinterestedness, a freedom from determinate concepts and concerns. On Pascal's account, boredom survives in and is only masked by diversion. Time spent in diversion is dead time, empty time. The aesthetic consciousness, in contrast, enjoys an experience of plenitude, and of a kind of timelessness achieved without fleeing temporality in the pursuit of some conceptual abstraction.

Consequently, the "disinterestedness" that Kant and Schiller described in their philosophical writings is not to be confused or conflated with the lack of interest that distinguishes boredom as a typically unpleasant experience. The pleasure taken in the beautiful ought to be conceived, in fact, as a cure for this condition, encounters with the beauty of art and of nature serving as an antidote for boredom. Yet the vagueness of these categories, rather frequently noted here, precludes any oversimplified contrasts. Schiller's exalted, even hyperbolic claims about the transforming power of the *Spieltrieb* need to be read in conjunction with Kierkegaard's warnings about the seductive dangers of aesthetic experience—indeed, its potential as diversion. And while the superficially bored, "fidgety" psyche easily contrasts with the balanced, disinterested consciousness portrayed by Schiller in his letters, the latter is not so readily distinguished from the third and deepest level of boredom that Heidegger identified. This profound condition is not merely a boredom with some determinate this or that, but rather a "queer kind of indifference" that draws everything into itself, and one that induces a certain feeling of timelessness.

Some readers, once again, will worry about using the word *boredom* to designate anything other than a negative experience. I want only at this point to recapitulate the insight that Heidegger, Pascal, and the mystics have all so convincingly articulated: this deep form of boredom is potentially revelatory. In the same dark night of the human spirit, two paths can be discerned, perhaps diverging from a common source, one leading to despair, the other to equanimity and freedom.

Moreover, these various forms of disinterest can be understood in diverse ways, as labile states of consciousness or as more enduring psychic dispositions. The possible relations among them need to be conceived as similarly diverse, and not entirely in terms of criteria of sameness, that is, in terms of how one might be said to *resemble* the other. It is also important to ask how one might be perceived as causing or precipitating another, so that my boredom with a particular object or activity might spark the search for some diversion, but might also evolve into a more general and positive form of disinterest—an open, contemplative attitude. Boredom thwarts play, but as Kierkegaard clearly understood, it can also inspire or stimulate playful activity. This latter, of course, can take the form of a play-as-work best symbolized by the frenzied tourist. It can also take the form of a frivolous and irresponsible activity that altogether and permanently removes the player from the realm of ethical and religious decision making. Yet, despite Kierkegaard's legitimate concerns, boredom can also have a purgative effect, even a liberating effect, freeing a person from the bondage of determinate objects or concerns. In this way, boredom can be regarded as a *praeparatio* for aesthetic enjoyment, or for religious contemplation.

My purpose here has been neither to recommend the theories of aesthetic judgment formulated by Kant and Schiller nor to reject them—but rather to maintain a posture *indeterminate* with respect to particular evaluations of their philosophical perspectives on this issue! It is altogether plausible that one might be able to account for certain judgments of taste in ways that do not involve the concept of disinterestedness as a central or even a necessary feature of the explanation.[34] The Kantian assumption that human beings are a sufficiently homogeneous collection of organisms (possessing a "common sense") so as to respond in a similar fashion to beautiful objects (his transcendental deduction of pure judgments of taste) is one that may or may not be supported by empirical evidence. Yet insofar as at least some instances of aesthetic enjoyment are characterized, perhaps even facilitated, by an attitude of disinterestedness, the logical link with both the concept of boredom and various ideals of religious indifference is preserved, and the accounts of both Kant and Schiller remain worthy of attention here. Those accounts clarify the nature of disinterestedness as a freedom from determinacy, not a freedom from all interests, but a freedom from any particular interest—quintessentially, a freedom to play.

This is the freedom that Schiller saw actualized in aesthetic contemplation, the same freedom that Charles Peirce described as necessary for "Musement." Peirce coined this term in 1908, in his essay sketching a "neglected" argument for the reality of God. When later pressed by Lady (Victoria) Welby to supply a more detailed account of the nature and origins of his concept of Musement, Peirce reported it to be "thoroughly soaked" by Schiller's *Spieltrieb*.[35] Now Peirce's remark should not be interpreted as casual. Even upon a brief inspection, the two conceptions display a significant resemblance.

First and most obvious is the fact that Peirce portrayed Musement as "Pure Play," a "lively exercise" of one's powers of observation and reflection, having no specific purpose and obeying no rules, other than the one "law of liberty."[36] This portrayal depicts as essential to Musement the same sort of disinterestedness and freedom from determinacy that characterize Schiller's *Spieltrieb*. Moreover, Peirce like Schiller understood this playful mode of thought to be one that quite typically takes the form of aesthetic contemplation. Of course, such contemplation can prove in the long run to be morally edifying, as Schiller noticed with his assertion that it is "only out of the aesthetic . . . state that the moral can develop."[37] On Peirce's account, even when Musement "flowers" into moral reflection or religious meditation, nevertheless, it retains something of its character as aesthetic. This helps to explain why Peirce was convinced that the Muser, when reflecting upon the nature and evolution of the universe, would eventually discover the hypothesis about God's reality to be "attractive."

Indeed, Musement is a kind of hypothetical thinking, a playing with ideas, neither the affirming or rejecting of specific beliefs and concepts, but rather a having of all beliefs "as though one did not have them." In more technical terms, Musement is a species of *abduction*; for Peirce, this is the mode of inference involved in the generation of hypotheses, as such, to be distinguished from both deductive and inductive reasoning.[38] In abduction, a particular observed instance or "case" is contemplated from the perspective supplied by some general idea or "law." Similarly, on Schiller's view, of the two contrasting impulses that are harmonized in play, one furnishes "cases" (*"Falle"*), the other gives "laws" (*"Gesetze"*).[39] Abduction, then, at least the sort employed in the exercise of Musement, is a form of cognitive play, a playing with ideas, perceptions, and feelings, with various configurations of them, and with the candidate hypotheses that might render them meaningful.

Abduction is a process of hypothesis formation, but

in order to grasp its full significance it is necessary to understand "hypothesis" here in a very general sense. A hypothesis is an explanation. It lends intelligibility to multifarious perceptions. It supplies the defining "cause" for a multiplicity of effects. Judgments like "X is dangerous" or "X is good" or "X loves me" are, in fact, hypotheses that unify and render meaningful the various details of any experience or set of observations. They apply to specific observed cases certain law-like beliefs about the typical characteristics of dangerous or of good things, of loving persons or of the experience of being loved.

Such hypotheses entail those observation-statements that combine and cooperate to suggest their plausibility. (So that if "X is dangerous," it would be the case that X displays certain distinctive characteristics.) But neither these observations nor the hypothesis needs to be articulated explicitly; nor, frequently, can they be, as in the case of an explosive, incommunicable insight that organizes and illuminates a vague and confused "buzz" of perceptions. The connection between observations and hypotheses is not a necessary one (like the deductive link between premises and conclusion) and it cannot be defined in terms of statistical probabilities (as in induction). Hypotheses can be deductively explicated and inductively tested, but they are generated and entertained abductively, a unique mode of inference so fundamental to human thought that it is involved in every perceptual act.[40]

Abductive inferences may be unconscious and seemingly indubitable, as when I simply perceive something *as* something. On the other hand, the abductive insight may result from a complex series of thought experiments involving the imaginative arrangement and rearrangement of observed facts, the foregrounding and suppressing of particular details, the connecting and disconnecting of specific characteristics, and the "playing with" or entertaining of attractive hypotheses. It is this latter form of abduction that Peirce identified as Musement.

Consequently, in complex abductive inferences, observed phenomena are arranged and rearranged to fit the patterns of meaning that are generated by specific inductively established beliefs or "rules." These beliefs are also "played with," assembled into various combinations, relevant ones selected and others suppressed. In this fashion, objects and phenomena are classified or, as Peirce expressed it, a certain observed "result" will be grasped as an instance or "case" of some general "rule."[41] This sort of thing, I would propose, is what artworks, from the simplest metaphor to the most elaborate work of fiction, invite us to do: to classify and reclassify our experience, to test our beliefs and to entertain new ones; in short, to engage in Musement.

As with Kant, Schiller, and the spiritual writers, for Peirce the disinterestedness of Musement manifests itself as indeterminacy—here, an indeterminacy of the rules employed in abductive inference. These rules are indeterminate even where they exist ready at hand and can be easily articulated. Their indeterminacy consists, first of all, in the fact that their power is merely "suggestive" of some conclusion; by contrast with deduction, in abductive inferences no specific conclusion is necessarily entailed.[42] Moreover, Musement requires a "casting aside of all serious purpose" so that no concept or belief will be imposed by the Muser as an explanation in order to satisfy some preference or achieve some end. Rather, in Musement these beliefs literally come into play; they are themselves played with, tried on for size, always regarded hypothetically, as imagined possibilities. The process is contemplative, open or receptive to the thing being considered—as Peirce described it, fully "awake" to whatever might appear.

Musement can involve the imaginative trying out of existing rules of thought. But it is important to recognize the more radical instance of a playful inquiry that proceeds with the lack of any appropriate concepts or rules (an even greater indeterminacy). Here Musement is creative in the sense that it must generate new classifications, rather than simply engage in the imaginative process of trying out or testing existing ones to fit the case at hand. Often it is the strangeness of the case, its surprising or mysterious qualities, that will rule out these old categories of thought. Yet a cultivated indifference can also help to stimulate new perspectives on even the most everyday, ordinary phenomena. Here a conscious detaching of oneself from well-entrenched beliefs about such phenomena "makes room" for playful thinking.

Once again, this playful thinking can take a wide variety of forms. In the process of Musement, one can "try out" emotions as well as explanations, and these emotions can themselves have interpretive value. That is to say, one's emotional response to a thing or situation is part of what that thing or situation *means*. This sort of expanded, generous conception of what is involved in giving or having an interpretation is especially relevant to the task of sketching a semiotic of boredom. Quite typically, the bored person experiences a vacuum of meaning not in the sense of lacking any clear explanation or understanding of what is going on, but rather as the absence of any interest, enjoyment, or consolation associated with it. Of course, a total lack of understanding can also eventuate in boredom. And novel explanations or deeper understanding can bring about a new birth of interest, renewed enjoyment. So "interpretation" will be best conceived as a vague but complex category embracing a wide variety of cognitive, emotional, and behavioral responses to the thing being interpreted.

Peirce distinguished Musement as a "lively exercise" from any form of mere "reverie" in which the thinker is immersed in "vacancy" or "dreaminess." It may begin passively as a "drinking in" of impressions, but soon evolves into a more active attentiveness. Moreover, it culminates in the playful "give and take" of conversation with whatever presents itself to consciousness. Peirce's advice for the prospective Muser was relatively simple and straightforward: "With your eyes open, awake to what is about or within you, and open conversation with yourself; for such is all meditation."[43]

Compare Heidegger's insistence that meditative thought, while it involves a "kind of passivity," is "in no way a matter of weakly allowing things to slide and drift along."[44] In fact, it is most felicitous to conceive of such meditation as lying "beyond the distinction between activity and passivity." While activity and passivity require a willing to do or not to do this or that, meditative thinking "does not belong to the domain of will." It is better characterized as a form of *waiting*, a dispositional openness or readiness—in Heidegger's expression, a "releasement toward things" (*Die Gelassenheit zu den Dingen*).[45] Manifesting itself somewhat misleadingly as a form of passivity, nevertheless, within this releasement a "higher acting" is concealed.

The contrast just observed is one between Musement or meditative thinking and some purely empty or passive form of consciousness. It is one thing simply to "do nothing" or have "nothing in mind." It is another thing for a person to be aware that this nothing matters, embracing an infinitude of possible actions, possible meanings. Such a contrast presupposes another, however, one that Heidegger identified as the difference between "meditative" and "calculative" thinking. For Peirce, the contrast is explicated in terms of the distinction between abduction, as the essence of Musement, and deductive or inductive modes of reasoning.

I do not intend to provide here a lengthy analysis of Peirce's logic of inquiry (although a few additional details will need to be examined in the process of portraying that logic as semiotic). The most immediately relevant distinction to note is that between abduction and deduction, the latter governed rigidly by rules of inference that, when employed in a valid fashion, yield necessary conclusions. Recall, at this point, Rahner's

101

characterization of the logic that pervades Ignatius's spiritual exercises as being something other than "the logic of a deductive ethics of general principles." Rather, it is more akin to the rules that govern "make believe," the sort employed in a "play-acting experiment."[46] This is the abductive logic of Musement.

It is also the logic of indifference, since both Peirce and Rahner insisted that the individual properly engaged in such an exercise will have achieved a certain detachment from determinate beliefs and desires, especially those that fuel expectations about the meditation itself, the manner it which it ought to progress, the sort of result that it ought to yield. This is the detachment necessary for play, and an important ingredient of any successful process of experimentation.[47] Biased toward no particular result, the disinterested person will be capable of discerning the correct result, will be ready for it, like a "balance at equilibrium."

Such talk about playful thought, about meditation as a calm but "lively exercise," can belie the very real suffering that might be involved in achieving the detachment that is its prerequisite. In an appropriate state of "readiness," one must be prepared to embrace possible outcomes in sharp conflict with what one most desires. Time and change can exacerbate this difficulty. What manifests itself as pleasing in the present moment can vanish in the next, to be replaced, as the spiritual writers repeatedly remind us, by the darkest desolation. Death is an important subject for meditation in the religious traditions precisely because this awareness of the inevitability of death, including the "death" of each passing moment, breeds a certain attitude of detachment, frequently enough, with suffering as its midwife.

Play does not preclude struggle. Indifference need not be cold or anaesthetic, requiring the absence of all feeling. Otherwise, it would make no sense to describe love as "disinterested." To love X disinterestedly is not the same thing as having no interest in X; that would be no love at all. It is a matter of detaching oneself from selfish desires and interests, loosening the rigid bonds of preconception and standard expectation, renouncing all "property rights" with respect to the beloved. It is a matter of loving X for its own sake or, in certain theistic contexts, loving all things for God's sake, continuously mindful of their utter gratuity.

Considered from the perspective being sketched here, indifference should never be understood as equivalent to the ignoring of real differences. The achievement of indifference does not require the admission that my interest in one thing is no different from my interest in any other thing. On the contrary, it facilitates a deeper and more nuanced awareness of whatever one really does encounter in experience, through detachment from potentially distorting beliefs and biases. At the same time, it manifests itself as an equanimity of the sort that Saint Paul described when he reported to the Philippians: "I have learned, in whatever state I am, to be content. I know how to be abased and I know how to abound; in any and all circumstances I have learned the secret of facing plenty and hunger, abundance and want. I can do all things in him who strengthens me."[48]

For one who has learned Paul's "secret," the logic of indifference will be embodied in powerful habits of thought and feeling. Such a person will be prepared for both joy and sorrow, for either ecstasy or boredom, clinging to neither, rejecting neither, always remaining attentive to what each experience conveys, what each signifies.

4

RITUAL, REDUNDANCY, AND THE RELIGIOUS IMAGINATION

IF VARIETY is the spice of life, then one might conclude that redundancy is a recipe for boredom. Constantly repeated behavior is habit forming, and habitual behavior is generally regarded as boring. Psychologist Mihalyi Csikszentmihalyi has explicitly associated habit responses in the individual and redundancy in the environment with the experience of boredom.[1] Abraham Maslow argued that the habitual, ritualistic behavior of persons who engage in the practices of organized religious communities virtually negates the possibility that such individuals will achieve religious "peak-experiences."[2] Samuel Beckett added an existential flavor to this psychological critique of the habitual. In an essay on Proust, he noted the latter's remark that "if there were no such thing as Habit, life would of necessity appear delicious to all those whom death would threaten at every moment, that is to say, all Mankind."[3] Here, Beckett described habit as "the guarantee of a dull inviolability"; boredom is the necessary result of habit's "adequate performance," a boredom that prevents one from perceiving the depth of meaning in human experience, at the same time that it insulates against suffering.

Nevertheless, for Charles Peirce and for the medieval scholastics who influenced his thinking on this topic, habits can sometimes be regarded as skills or abilities, not stultifying in their effects, but having a vital impact both on physical and on cognitive activity. Thoroughly ingrained habits constitute an individual's "second nature" and lift that individual beyond a crude and highly limited natural state. For example, it is the person who speaks French "habitually" who can do creative things with that language, and not the struggling student who has just begun to learn it. So, too, we are likely to be aesthetically pleased by the performance of an actor who thoroughly knows his role and his lines and is thus free to perform, not burdened with the task of having, consciously, to think about each thing that he has to do or say. His performance is creative and entertaining, but it is also habitual; that is, it is second nature to him.

Of course, it is entirely possible that a performance

can become habitual to the point of being stale. There are enough examples of a "killing" redundancy to suggest that the concepts of habit and redundancy are, from the point of view relevant to this inquiry, thoroughly ambiguous. As with good and bad boredom, the distinction between good and bad redundancy is a matter of interpretation. Redundancy is a source of security, comfort. A calm person breathes slowly and regularly. A healthy heartbeat is steady and strong. The experimental method presupposes redundancy. It is essential to pedagogy and discipline. Practice makes perfect, and practice typically requires repetition. Even so, the dangers associated with redundancy in education, or in various forms of athletic and musical training, have frequently been noted as well.[4] Constant repetition poses the risk not only of physical exhaustion, but of psychic fatigue in a variety of forms, most of which can quite accurately be regarded as species of boredom.

The experience of boredom frequently manifests itself as a heightened awareness of the redundancy of time itself. *Toujours la même chose;* one moment passes after another, no different from the one that preceded it or the one to follow. This absence of *difference,* a thick blanket of sameness that covers meaning and suffocates interest, is the distinguishing feature of time experienced as an oppressive void. Such a time must be killed before it kills, so that strategies of diversion quite typically incorporate the search for novelty, variety.

I do not intend to suggest that repetitive behavior is to be evaluated as "good" or "bad" exclusively in terms of whether or not it eventuates in an experience of boredom. Boredom is frequently the sort of thing that one expects and is expected to put up with; and the inability to tolerate even a mild or temporary tedium should be regarded as a sign of emotional immaturity rather than of creative genius. The boredom of much repetitive practice is readily endured as a prelude to the satisfaction of employing those practiced skills in a game or a contest or a performance. The person who struggles to circumvent every experience of boredom achieves little, and quickly drowns in a sea of meaning-less diversions.

I am less interested in the fact that redundancy some-times precipitates boredom than in the more complex fact that sometimes it does, while sometimes it does not. This is most certainly true of the repetition prescribed for religious ritual, designed to deepen religious emotion and commitment, but sometimes having a very differ-ent and deadening effect. How can one account for this difference?[5]

At the outset, I want to argue that the issue of cau-sality can be entirely misconceived so that, in some instances, the elements of redundancy and variety in behavior (or the environment) are ascribed a causal efficacy that they simply do not possess. That is to say, boredom in its most profound (and philosophically in-teresting) manifestations has the character of a powerful psychic disposition. As previously noted, this sort of deeply rooted boredom does not attach to particular objects, activities, or circumstances. Since it is not simply a boredom with "this or that," it is unlikely to be cured by less of "this or that" through the substitu-

108

tion of an alternative stimulus; nor is it likely that such boredom was caused by too much "this or that" in the first place.

Indeed, one of the sad ironies exposed by the great philosophers of boredom is their insight that persons can rush to treat with large overdoses of variety a boredom that they mistakenly assumed to have been caused by the terrible sameness of their experience. But since their diagnosis was faulty, the proposed cure is at best a placebo. One can travel to a great many exotic and faraway places, masking one's boredom, carrying it along like a suitcase. Similarly, a marriage can be so thoroughly poisoned by ennui that no amount of change (move to a new home, shift in careers, the decision to become parents, endless variation in sexual postures and technique) can serve as antidote, restoring intimacy and excitement. So, too, in the case of spiritual dryness or of acedia, a change in liturgical rubrics, in the method or subject matter of meditation, is likely to have only a temporary and superficial effect, alleviating religious boredom altogether only in the most superficial of cases.

This important caveat notwithstanding, the relationship between redundancy, habit formation, and boredom deserves attention from anyone concerned with evaluating boredom as a religiously significant phenomenon. The element of redundancy is ubiquitous in religious practices, sometimes involving the repetition of certain general patterns of thought, speech, and behavior, while allowing for moderate variety, often determined by differences in the season, time of day, or particular

occasion. In extreme examples, redundancy is a defining feature of the practice, its key structural element,
as in the Roman Catholic recitation of the rosary, or
Hindu *japam*, with the constant repetition of a mantra.

Now one of the basic principles of information theory stipulates that the amount of *information* embodied
in a communication event increases with an increase
in entropy, variety, or uncertainty. Correspondingly, the
greater the redundancy, the less information there is to
be processed. To supply a simple example: The repetition of the definite article "the" typed fifty times on
a page communicates less information than a descriptive paragraph containing the same number of words.
Similarly, one could double the size of the descriptive
paragraph by typing every word in it twice, without
yielding any increase in the level of information that it
contains.

It is tempting to leap from this sort of rudimentary
analysis to the easy conclusion that "high redundancy"
is equivalent to "low information," and that the latter
is a recipe for boredom. But this conclusion would be
problematic for a number of reasons. In the first place,
no easy equation between "information" and "meaning" is possible, so that a tiny amount of information
could prove to be enormously meaningful (because of
the way that one evaluates it, its relevance to immediate circumstances, its relationship to other things that
one knows and cares about, and so on). In an altogether
different situation, it is possible that one might be
flooded with useless and relatively meaningless bits of
information. "The pattern is the thing."[6] That is to say,

redundancy is to be valued insofar as it generates *patterns of meaning* in human experience. It is entirely possible that an exposure to redundancy could occasion the discovery or rebirth of meaning, while high-information states can yield a numbing boredom.

The latter case is best explained by the observation that some of the variety in information is *noise* (I use the word here in the technical sense employed by communication theorists to denote anything that corrupts a signal, obscures the meaning of a sign, or prevents its effective interpretation).[7] If one were to attend to all of the information embedded in any given situation or communication event, much potential meaning would quickly be drowned in noise. Redundancy in information and habit responses in the individual function as suppressors, muffling the noise, allowing meaningful patterns of information to emerge in consciousness and to be interpreted. The fact that this redundancy and these habitual responses can also precipitate the experience of boredom suggests that boredom itself has the potentially useful effect of serving as an information filter.[8] This is a boredom-as-fatigue, a numbness that protects against the pain of excessive stimuli. The necessity of discernment is once again exposed by these deliberations, since it appears that boredom can either save meaning from an overdose of information or enshroud meaning in a numbing indifference. (Beckett was worried about the latter possibility when he warned about a boredom that masks psychic pain, saving us from suffering at the cost of inducing an "existential" blindness.)

111

Such considerations notwithstanding, I will continue to refer to the psychic condition of being bored as a "low-information state," indicating a deficit of meaningful information. One can exist in such a state even while being situated in a high-information environment. Two explanations of how this might be so have already been suggested: in the first place, not all information will be evaluated by an individual as meaningful and, in the second, a considerable amount of information might be filtered out or suppressed. These explanations are not necessarily unrelated, since judgments about the poor quality or irrelevance of certain information might supply the motivation to suppress it as noise. Suppression can be a conscious act of selective attention, a decision that certain information constitutes a "distraction" and ought best to be ignored. It stands to reason that these judgments will gradually become embodied in habitual responses and that a good deal of the filtering process will become automatic.

There is a third potential explanation of how one might become or remain bored in a high-information environment. In this scenario, bored individuals are simply incapable of processing the meaningful information to which they are exposed. Consider the example of a woman listening to a lively conversation about matters of vital importance to her, but one conducted in a language that she does not understand. Interest might be sustained by her awareness that the conversation is, in fact, of great significance. The listener might then struggle to identify any meaningful signs, occasional words that have cognates in her native language, changes in tone of voice, or facial expressions if she is in the physical presence of the speakers. If the conversation is not framed by an awareness of its importance, however, the continuous stream of indecipherable utterances is likely soon to be perceived as meaningless babble, causing the listener to become bored unless she is able to amuse herself with some alternative stimulus. (The latter is a common enough occurrence, which is why boring lectures—sometimes on highly technical matters that one does not fully understand— are often perfect occasions for daydreaming.)

Boredom can be conceived as a kind of "semiotic breakdown" when the primary cause of its occurrence is judged to be an *incapacity*, a person's inability to interpret the meaningful information embodied in a given situation. This incapacity sometimes can be analyzed as a lack of skill, like the lack of linguistic ability in the example just explored. But one might also fail to learn what is meaningful in a conversation, sinking gradually into boredom, because one is hard of hearing or completely deaf.[9] This is a different kind of incapacity, one that might be compensated for or corrected, but not through the acquisition of a particular skill or expertise. (I will want to consider religious analogues for both of these types of incapacity, while at the same time, from a certain pragmatic perspective, blurring the distinction between them.)

It is also entirely possible that semiotic breakdown might be caused, not by the interpreter's lack of skill, but by an excess of noise in the environment. One fails to process the relevant information (is unable to do so) because of the noise. (Again, I refer to "noise" here in the technical sense supplied by information theory, but this does not preclude the possibility of noise in the ordinary sense, the latter being sufficient to account for semiotic breakdown in a conversation.) This possibility is related to the earlier explanation involving the suppression of noise, but with a different emphasis. Here meaningful information is lost in the noise, rather than information perceived *as* noise being intentionally or habitually muffled.

Finally, one can imagine the case of a person who is capable of perceiving what is meaningful in a communication and undistracted by any noise. Nevertheless, such an individual chooses not to attend to the meaningful information. If the result is boredom, then it seems appropriate to say that such a person chooses to be bored, doing nothing to prevent it, failing to attend to matters of interest. In the spiritual life, this sort of choosing, of failing to attend, constitutes the sin of acedia. If the choice is motivated by extreme fatigue, however, judgments about the quality of volition and the seriousness of sin are likely to become murky.

Even in the case of someone choosing to ignore meaningful information, it might be appropriate to analyze semiotic breakdown in terms of a perceived incapacity. There is a sense, after all, in which vice can be regarded as a kind of moral inaptitude, spiritual sloth, or sluggishness representing a certain weakness of will. This, once again, is why judgments about acedia can be problematic and require discernment. Fatigue is inevitable, the need for rest likewise so, and I have already suggested that boredom can signal that need for rest, a natural response to the stimulus of excessive information. The judgment that Samson or the disciples in Gethsemane are somehow blameworthy when they succumb to drowsiness presupposes that both boredom and fatigue can be resisted. Moreover, in some cases when an individual appears incapable of offering such resistance, that incapacity itself is to be evaluated as a symptom of moral failure.

Consider the likelihood of a coach displaying irritation rather than sympathy toward an athlete who is unable to perform effectively due to poor conditioning. Weakness of will or the incapacity to attend to what is spiritually meaningful, in a similar fashion, can be attributed to a failure to persist in spiritual exercises. This much is old news. Now the analytical spotlight needs to be focused on the element of redundancy in such practices, its role in habit formation, and the effect of such habits on the quality of experience.

The sketch of an explanation has already been supplied for my observation that redundancy is both an important ingredient of religious ritual and a factor contributing to the boredom that can afflict ritual participants. High redundancy signals a reduced level of information. The effect on practitioners can be beneficial when this reduction involves the suppression of potentially distracting noise. The consequence is more likely to be a greater vulnerability to boredom when high redundancy corresponds simply to a deficit of meaningful information. In the latter case, habit responses induced by repetition have a deadening effect on human awareness, becoming the "guarantee of a dull inviolability." In the former instance, habit is perceived to have a liberating effect on the interpretive process, enhancing attention, reducing distraction, and facilitating the flow of information.[10]

This sketchy account requires amplification in order to serve the purposes of my inquiry. Consider, first, how redundancy generates the expectation that some constantly repeated pattern of events will continue to occur in the future. Now this expectancy is, in fact, the essence of habit, influencing how an individual will respond to a familiar configuration of stimuli, under recognizable circumstances. Insofar as redundancy helps to generate expectations, it plays a vital role in the formation of habits. As redundancy proceeds to confirm expectations, it both activates and strengthens those habitual responses.

Powerful habits are automatic and often unconscious tendencies to behave in a certain general way in specific situations. As conditioned responses to the redundant features of experience, they do not require one's constant, conscious attention. Figuratively speaking, habit clears "space" in consciousness, since one need not be preoccupied with the regular, redundant features of experience. This economizing power of habit can have diverse, even contrasting effects.

Notice, for example, that *habit liberates attention,* frees consciousness to discover new sources or types of information. It is in this respect that habit is an essential precondition for all creative activity, as redundancy supplies a background against which various and diverse bits of information can be discerned, playfully manipulated, and perceived as meaningful.

It cannot be determined in advance, of course, that a liberated attention will immediately or necessarily seek to engage new stimuli or, if it does, that the results will be creative discoveries rather than random diversions. Neither is it the case that these are the only two possibilities to consider. Habitual behavior is often unconscious behavior. But a consciousness thus "emptied" by the effects of habit may remain precisely in that condition. I would argue, in fact, that this is one of the goals of certain religious ritual and meditative practices. More accurately, religious practices are designed for a variety of purposes, several of which may require the achievement of this "empty-minded" state, and some of which may require that the devotee persist in that condition.

While Marx's portrayal of religion as an "opiate" may be criticized as a caricature and as hyperbole, it certainly seems reasonable to assert that many religious rituals have a comforting effect, not by accident but by design.[11] These rituals help participants to feel more secure in a vast universe of constant change that may otherwise threaten to overwhelm them with anxiety. Here the feature of redundancy in ritual plays an essential role, precisely because it works to generate a whole pattern of expectations. Redundancy breeds familiarity, security. Every parent shares this insight who has tried to calm an agitated infant with the rhythmic rocking of a chair, gently repeated pats on the back, or the soft humming of a familiar tune. I am not suggesting that all religious ritual has this function or even that this is ritual's primary function. Nevertheless, it seems obvious that many persons turn to religion as a source of comfort and that the organized redundancy of certain religious practices is a factor helping to explain why they often find what they are looking for. (The systems of meaning supplied by religious belief and the membership in a nurturing religious community are, of course, other such factors.)

This is another way of portraying redundancy as a weapon for combating noise. Noise can be an important source of anxiety, so that one can imagine how the agitated infant might have become frightened in the first place by a loud and unfamiliar noise. The use of redundancy can be an effective method (to put it most simply) for calming the mind. Calmness of mind is obviously valuable for a variety of religious purposes, most notably, for the manner in which it facilitates prayer and meditation. The calm, empty consciousness is one free to engage in religious contemplation, to direct its attention, now liberated, to various spiritual goods. But I want to suggest that this purpose should not conceal from view another potentially quite important religious objective, which is the contemplation of, indeed, the subsisting in, that very emptiness. In the terms supplied by my earlier analysis, redundancy can be a training method for the cultivation of religious indifference. And the emptiness that is achieved when habit and redundancy have worked their noise-clearing effects can be a sign with considerable religious meaning.

It is no easy task to explain how a state of virtually

"zero information" could be religiously meaningful, but a good deal of the discourse of mysticism and of negative theology has been directed to that end. My far less ambitious purpose here is simply to observe that it is not always a religious desideratum to fill up this empty state with new bits of information. To be sure, a mind thus calmed may very well be poised to achieve a fuller awareness of phenomena previously inaccessible to experience (much as a person may gradually become aware of objects in a dimly lit room once her vision has made the adjustment, has become habituated, to the darkness there). Nevertheless, this seems to be a possibility for which one must be *ready*, rather than an outcome that one can manipulate.

At the same time, one must be ready for nothing to occur and for the possibility of boredom. While habit can liberate attention, it can also place one in bondage to an overpowering tedium. This psychic state of "having nothing consciously to do" can be experienced as leisure, both stimulating and refreshing. But the sense that there is "nothing to do" manifests itself commonly enough as a feeling of being trapped by boredom. The difference between these two possibilities is a difference of interpretation; that is, a matter of how one interprets a particular psychic condition. I have tried to suggest that this process of interpretation is not one over which the interpreter can exercise perfect control. Further, I have proposed that either possible outcome is one that can be evaluated as having a religious significance.

It is possible to control, within reason, the manner in which one directs attention, the sort of activity in which one engages. It seems probable that a redundancy to which I freely and happily submit is less likely to contribute to my being bored than one to which I am subjected against my will (for example, a traffic jam). Once bored, I can also control my attention, resisting or succumbing to whatever might distract me from this tedious state of affairs. I might be grateful for the fantasy or the music that helps me to endure the time stuck in traffic. Of course, the distractions that permit me to "endure" religious devotions or time spent with a loved one are a bit more troubling. Wherever my attention is, (at least for the time being) there is my treasure.

IT IS NOT reason or proof, but habit, Pascal argued, that plays the most decisive role in religious conversion. He was so impressed by the power of habit that he advised unbelievers seeking faith to behave "just as if they did believe, taking holy water, having masses said, and so on."[12] Since "custom is our nature," he explained, "anyone who grows accustomed to faith believes it." A belief grounded in complex argumentation is fragile, requiring, if it is to survive, that these arguments be constantly, consciously reviewed and rehearsed. On the other hand, habit is the precondition and source of an "easier belief," one that works unconsciously, "leading" the mind and shaping human inclinations.[13]

If Pascal's analysis suggests that there is a continuity between habit and belief, with Peirce that connection is made explicit since he was convinced that all "belief is of the nature of a habit."[14] A belief is that upon which a person is prepared to act; it has the potential to shape

120

human conduct, sometimes but not necessarily in a conscious fashion. Consequently, I might have a great many beliefs, influencing my thought and behavior, of which I am not fully aware.[15] The very fact that certain beliefs operate below the level of awareness, is the key to the great power that they can exercise over human life, a power that can be tapped and utilized. My habits control me, but I can also control my habits to some degree. The effort expended in cultivating specific habits is of vital importance since these habits, in any given situation and to a greater extent than any set of conscious deliberations, are likely to determine my actual behavior.

Except in those cases that involve the sudden conversion to a new way of acting, thinking, or being, redundancy is the most reliable and effective method of habit formation. Pascal was especially concerned about the relationship between habits thus formed and human volition, in much the same way that Peirce emphasized in his philosophy the extraordinary significance of "self-control."[16] But it is difficult to know exactly how one ought to describe this relationship. On the one hand, it makes sense to say that volition can be strengthened through the acquisition of habits, so that one can actually "practice" volition or "train" the will. On the other hand, this same process may be described as one that, through the influence of habit, makes the power of will unnecessary. Having conditioned myself to behave in a certain determinate way under certain determinate circumstances, I now experience as automatic what once involved a struggle.

Nevertheless, in all likelihood that struggle was necessary for achieving my present state of affairs. Typically, it is the repeated exercise of the will, the constant bending of the will in a determinate way under specific conditions, that results in this later experience of ease. And so volition can play a vital role in habit formation, even if one prefers to say that the will is not actively engaged in shaping human conduct once habit has taken over.

Admittedly, this portrayal of the relationship between habit and will is something of a caricature. Not all habits are consciously, intentionally formed in the sense that they are patterns of behavior that one has struggled to cultivate. One can "fall into" certain habits, as is frequently the case with those regarded as undesirable or as vices. While specific, discrete actions may have been performed intentionally, even repeated intentionally, it may never have been intended that such action become habitual. There is a slippery-slope phenomenon here, a risk involved whenever I agree to do or even to think something, while rejecting the judgment that I am the sort of person who would typically act or think that way. I can find myself trapped in certain patterns of behavior, changed, in some respects "against my will," and yet I am also partially responsible for being in this condition.[17]

There is a second potential distortion in the sketch supplied above of the relation between habit and volition. Many habits are not so powerful that they eliminate all space or need for the operation of the will. Rather, they are experienced as "gentle" forces, behavioral tendencies or inclinations; while they give form to human thought and conduct, they do not act as perfectly rigid constraints on volition. It is more accurate to describe human activity, quite frequently, as being shaped by the interplay of habit with the will, much as the artist freely shapes the material with which she is working, but only in patterns to which that material will conform. Habit can determine the general character of human activity, while yet leaving it open, on any particular occasion, to further determination.

It would seem reasonable to expect that the greater the redundancy in behavior, the more solidly will habits become entrenched, affording less opportunity for the exercise of volition. Where repetition is just sufficient to establish order and security, to generate patterns of meaning, but without becoming the dominant feature of an activity, room for freedom and creativity is preserved. These conclusions appear to be valid in the religious domain, where constant repetition and the habit that it breeds can in fact produce a "dull inviolability," not a cultivated sense of spiritual security, but a tedium that draws everything around it into the fog of sleep. On the other hand, some variety in ritual performance, the opportunity for spontaneous and creative behavior, are factors that can reduce the risk of boredom even as they enliven religious experience.

As reasonable as these conclusions might appear on the surface (and as accurate as they might be in specific cases), the phenomena under consideration are more complex than they would indicate. In fact, specifically religious phenomena provide some of the most startling counterevidence to these claims, whenever extreme redundancy is both prescribed and experienced as a prelude to religious ecstasy. In evaluating such evidence, once again, the question is raised about how religious sensibilities can be stimulated rather than deadened by repetitive religious practices. I have already begun to answer that question by exploring some of the positive effects of exposure to redundancy (in terms of the suppression of noise, liberation of attention, and so on). Those earlier results need now to be reconsidered as details of a more general account of the relationship between habit and the human imagination. (I want to argue that boredom represents a certain failure of the imagination, but my treatment of this "failure" will prove to be as ambiguous as my treatment of the concept of boredom itself.)

I should confess before proceeding that my use of the word *imagination* in this discussion is also quite vague; no specific philosophical theory of the imagination is presupposed in these remarks. I share Wittgenstein's suspicion that the analogy between imagination and sense perception, as distinct but comparable mental processes, is dangerously misleading.[18] Talk about imagining as a kind of "seeing with the mind's eye" only generates confusion; it fuels the temptation to talk further about mental "images" as faint copies of sense impressions, but there is little evidence that such a perspective is accurate or that such a way of speaking is felicitous.

My general agreement with Wittgenstein on this issue notwithstanding, I want to acknowledge that the imagination is involved in every act of perception, that "seeing" itself requires "imagining."[19] In the terms supplied by a Peircean semiotic, one could make this same point by insisting that all experience is interpreted experience, with the implicit assumption that interpretation necessarily involves the constructive power of the imagination. The description of boredom as a failure of the imagination, then, is equivalent to my earlier characterization of it as a kind of semiotic breakdown. This failure is always already an *interpretive* failure—either the refusal or the inability to discover meaning in a thing or situation, to perceive it as interesting.

What I am proposing, without developing the suggestion in any great theoretical detail, is that every abductive inference involves the exercise of imagination. In the case of ordinary sense perception, what Peirce regarded as the "limit case" of abduction, these inferences are automatic and unconscious, the imagination being constrained by both habit and sense data.[20] Yet even in such cases, the results of inference are not completely and necessarily determined (as in deduction). When I perceive a thing I am not "free" to perceive it *as* anything that I choose or wish it to be. Nevertheless, the thing is never simply "given" to me in perception, so that it is altogether the case that I will have had to learn at some point how to perceive it as that particular thing rather than as some other. Moreover, my perception will be shaped by a variety of factors, including not only the status of my sense organs and my physical location in space and time, but my language, culture, education, and so forth. These latter are the source of many of the belief-habits that govern my everyday, ongoing semiotic exchanges with the world of sense objects. And those habits are the rules by which my imagination plays.

Wittgenstein observed that acts of imagination are "subject to the will" in a way in which much ordinary sense perception is not.[21] Yet this distinction is imperfect, since the process of imagining (even in the form of pure fantasy or daydreaming) will always be influenced by a great many factors (including habits of cognition) and so not entirely subject to the will.[22] Furthermore, there is a fundamental indeterminateness that characterizes ordinary perception, suggesting, once again, that the imagination is integrally involved even in such cases; that is to say, acts of recognition are always also acts of imaginative construal. Some simple examples can help to expose this quality of "indeterminateness" in each type of case, when one's imagination operates either in the absence or in the presence of a thing.

Habits will typically determine that a result be of a certain general character. If I am instructed to "imagine a flower," my general belief-habits about flowers will inevitably affect how I proceed. But whether I imagine a lilac or a rose, a flower violet or white or crimson in color, large or small, single or in a bunch, these characteristics of what I imagine are not rigidly determined by my beliefs. I can even combine features of one type of flower with the qualities of another to produce in my imagination one different from any species that I have ever observed in nature. My specific

126

purpose, the precise instructions that I am given, will obviously give direction to my imaginative play. A vast assortment of relevant beliefs will do likewise. Yet the exact result is not necessarily determined. That much freedom, as Schiller observed, is essential for play.

If someone directs my attention by asking me to "look at those flowers" in a neighbor's backyard, this indeterminateness, albeit mitigated, will persist as a quality of my experience. The meaning of my experience, the significance of what I see, is the product of an imaginative construction, which is not to say that it is a matter of pure fantasy or that I simply see whatever I choose to see. Rather, the imagination is involved in every application of a concept to a thing, or the linking of a "rule" to a "case" in the terms supplied by Peirce's logic of abduction.[23] That link is not the necessary connection that binds a particular conclusion to specific premises, as in deduction. The result of my looking, while inevitably shaped by actual sense data and by powerful habits of perception, is nevertheless indeterminate. I may know a good deal less about flowers than my companion does, for example, so that she may recognize them as orchids, whereas my experience is one of purple flowers only vaguely conceived, vaguely familiar.

Moreover, the full meaning of my experience is not determined exclusively by the belief-habits that constitute my stock of botanical knowledge. These flowers may remind me of the ones that my bride carried on our wedding day, or stimulate the recollection of time spent in Scotland several summers ago, or an experience from my childhood, or simply evoke vague feelings of sadness or gladness for reasons that I am unable to discern. Emotions, like conceptions, constitute my interpretive response to the flowers—are an integral part of what my experience of them means.

Ingrained habits of feeling, to be sure, shape those interpretive responses. It may be impossible for me to respond in any other way but with horror or disgust to the sight of a mangled corpse. And, on any given occasion, I may be unable to perceive an ocean sunset or the smiling face of my infant daughter as anything other than beautiful. Habits will typically have a gentler influence, however, manifesting themselves as vague tendencies to respond in a certain way to specific perceptual objects, but not rigidly determining that outcome. In fact, habits may conflict, compete with one another, so that the same image may evoke multiple and perhaps quite diverse responses. I may have a bittersweet recollection of my wedding day, or the trip to Scotland may be a happy memory that collides with the depressing one from my childhood (flowers at a funeral, perhaps). Consequently, my present sense perception can engage complex habits of feeling, all or several of which may constitute part of the meaning of that experience.

Finally, since my habits can change over time, so too can the nature of my interpretive responses to specific objects or phenomena. Religious exercises are often designed to effect this sort of change. Consider, as one example, Buddhist meditations on a decaying human corpse, meditations that are intended to diminish, eventually to eliminate, one's typical, habitual reactions to such an image, replacing them with a certain habit of detachment.[24] This sort of detachment is comparable to the one that a surgeon (or an undertaker) might have to achieve with respect to the human body in order to perform necessary tasks effectively. In each case a process of jading through habituation is utilized as a means of coming to perceive the body in a new way.

Being jaded is a species of boredom. Here it is assumed that being bored with something insofar as it is regarded from a given (standard) perspective permits our interest to be engaged by it in a different and more productive way. Still, the redundancy of constant exposure to the thing in question (in this example, human corpses) does not in itself guarantee the achievement of this new perspective. The risk of permanent jading can be quite real, so that the surgeon or the Buddhist practitioner might become afflicted by a blinding insensitivity, now experiencing only a cold indifference to human realities, rather than a felicitous sense of detachment that yields fresh insight.

I have observed the role that imagination plays in ordinary sense perception. The examples considered here suggest that imaginative play can be a rehearsal for future experiences, a practicing of many of the habits of thought, feeling, and conduct that will imbue those experiences with significance. Peirce understood the imagination to be just such a "laboratory" for the experimental development of useful habits of action.[25] His discussion of Musement explored how this experimental process might be played out in a religiously productive fashion. Habitual engagement in the practice of Musement can lead not only to the discovery but to the enhancement of a distinctive habit of perception, one involved in "recognizing" the universe as a living symbol of the divine reality. Similarly, Ignatius of Loyola prescribed a whole variety of imaginative exercises designed to arouse certain feelings and to stimulate particular ways of thinking. Their purpose was to strengthen in the exercitant dispositions that would shape future conduct, in a way judged desirable according to his Christian premises. Proper training in the imagination, he believed, can greatly increase the power of discernment needed to interpret and respond to one's everyday experiences.[26]

Perhaps engaging here in a redundant exercise can shed some light on the alleged religious efficacy of such practices. So at the risk of boredom (and with the hope for insight), I would invite the reader to review once again those effects that the repetitive features of a religious practice are intended to have on participants. In the first place, these regularities will frame the activity, organize it, helping to distinguish it from the noisy chaos of much of everyday life. As a consequence, novice practitioners will develop certain habits of thought and conduct, patterns of expectation that shape the activity; for the experienced participant these habits will be brought into play, strengthened and refined.

While delimiting the field of possible meanings for the religious activity, these habits also help to make meaning possible. That is why it is appropriate to describe habit as a gentle force providing some of the "rules" by which the religious imagination plays. By analogy, the rules of chess preclude all sorts of maneuvers as impermissible, while still allowing for an infinite variety of moves and strategies. Similarly, the possibilities of what a dance can "mean" are constrained not only by the dancer's practiced habits of movement, but by the sometimes not so gentle force of gravity itself.

I am constrained by what I know and believe, just as I am constrained by whom and what I love. We do not usually talk about being "trapped" by this sort of constraint, like being trapped in traffic or a tedious conversation. We do not typically worry about boredom as the natural precipitate of such a constraint. This is a constraint that, paradoxically, one can experience as freedom, a type of habit that one can recognize as skill. Gregory Bateson observed that "the better an organism 'knows' something, the less conscious it becomes of its knowledge, i.e., there is a process whereby knowledge (or 'habit'—whether of action, perception, or thought) sinks to deeper and deeper levels of the mind. This phenomenon, which is central to Zen discipline, is also relevant to all art and all skill."[27]

Habituation in the organism is comparable to automatization in some industrial process. The perceived value of this automatization consists in the greater productivity that it is designed to engender. No longer required to attend to those features of a task that are now performed automatically, the industrial worker is free to engage in some other activity (more or less relevant to the task itself, depending on how fully automatized the process of production has become).

It is a commonplace that such industrial work is all too frequently boring. (This is the other side of the coin, a freedom that can feel like a constraint.) It is boring for the same reason that habituation can reduce an organism to a dull state. While it is an essential precondition for the development of almost any useful skill— perceptual skills, fine and gross motor coordination, linguistic abilities, social and moral sensibilities, and so on—habituation results in "a lowering of the intensity of consciousness."[28] With the constant repetition of any experience, information processing can become fully automatic. That the resulting liberation of consciousness can be perceived paradoxically as an oppressive bondage to time, as a terrifying vacuum, is a fact that I have described as a failure of the imagination. No longer having to attend to this particular business at hand (because fully "automatized"), what more, one might try to imagine, is there to do?

The ability to perceive this "more," to recognize in any given situation or experience the potential for discovering new information, is a function of the imagination. "It is a sense . . . that there is always *more* to experience, and *more in* what we experience than we can predict. Without some such sense, even at the quite human level of there being something which deeply absorbs our interest, human life becomes perhaps not actually futile or pointless, but experienced as if it were. It becomes, that is to say, boring."[29] A person might fail to develop this imaginative ability altogether. It is also possible that, having developed this sense of the "more" in experience, a person might lose it, under certain conditions or for a duration of time. What is then lost must be understood as a semiotic capacity, the ability to perceive ordinary sense objects as signs, potentially rich in meaning. Of course, in order to be recognized *as* anything at all, in order to have any meaning whatsoever in experience, these objects must function as signs, that is, as objects of interpretation.

But it is one thing to interpret a sign and another thing to do so while also recognizing its character as a sign, its multivalence, its potential depth of meaning. Without the latter recognition there can only be a minimal significance to things; they can quickly become boring. "The loss, then, is the loss of ability to see *through* objects in the natural world to what lies beyond them. For the joyless, each thing is what it is and it suggests nothing further, no intimations of immortality or infinity. It is the imagination which supplies such hints, which treats the objects of sense as *potential symbols.*"[30]

Because this "more" is not something that one can predict, it stands to reason that gaining access to it is not something that one can easily control either. Imaginative skill is an important means of establishing such control. This skill is necessary for the recognition of anything as a sign of anything else. It is essentially an abductive skill, often displayed as the ability to rearrange and reconfigure old bits of information, to manipulate them playfully, creating or discovering new relationships, new insights. Play can be fun, alleviating boredom, but it helps to be good at playing; that is to say, play is something that one can fail at, fail to do well or to do at all.

At the risk of appearing to court the paradoxical, I want to suggest that there is a certain kind of failure that is essential to the success of imaginative play, and that this fact is most apparent in those cases where such play takes the form of religious meditation. Boredom can be a symptom of such failure, but I have already noted that from certain religious (and even philosophical) points of view, boredom is not always to be regarded a bad thing. The attempt to escape it too quickly is dangerous, diverting one from whatever it is that boredom can teach, can reveal.[31] My claim that the imagination must sometimes fail in order to succeed is intended to suggest that a diverted, overactive imagination can be a highly ineffective one.

The paradox here is no different from the one captured in Kant's talk about "purposiveness without a purpose," or in much of the religious discourse concerning disinterestedness. Clearly one might fail to discern the full religious significance of a particular thing or situation simply because of a lack of imagination, because of a dull imagination, perhaps caused by slothfulness, a failure to exercise it properly or with regularity. At the same time, the religious imagination has been portrayed as functioning most perfectly when it takes the form of an infinitely determinable "nought," detached and responsive to whatever appears. This is an imagination that plays with but never ignores its own limits. It is engaged in the contemplation of the sacred, posited as a reality that anything can potentially signify, but no image can adequately represent. Thus, it is an imagination that, in playing, must come to recognize the emptiness *(sunyata)* of its own images. The extreme redundancy of certain religious practices is intended to precipitate such a condition—in a sense, to empower the imagination by first reducing it to silence, to darkness.

5

BOREDOM, SEMIOSIS, AND SPIRITUAL EXERCISES

IT SHOULD not be at all surprising, given the general point of view adopted here, that boredom would be characterized as a semiotic phenomenon. Indeed, from a Peircean perspective, all human experience can be conceived as such—that is, as a continuous stream of semiosis.[1] In the experience of boredom that stream, the flow of meaningful information, has been reduced to a trickle; in rare cases, it has dried up altogether. This experience represents a failure to interpret some activity, thing, or situation *as* interesting.

I can sometimes control my experience of boredom by shifting attention from an object perceived as dull to something more engaging. This is a rather harmless diversion if the object is not judged worthy of my attention. In such a case, my failure will have no negative connotations. It is not an absolute failure to make any interpretation at all, but simply the failure to make a particular kind of interpretation; furthermore, in this instance, that particular kind of interpretation has been deemed inappropriate, or at least unnecessary.

Talk about semiotic breakdown, then, is not intended to suggest that boredom occurs only in those cases where the flow of information has been altogether disrupted. In such a case, one would experience the total absence of meaning, and consciousness would be reduced to the contemplation of a blank nothingness. This profound state of emptiness (itself interpretable in various ways) represents an extreme limit case of the phenomenon under consideration here. More typically, a bored person is able to make some sense out of a given experience, construes that experience as signifying something, yet that "something" is not judged to be of interest. Whatever that something is interpreted as being, it is not interpreted as being interesting.

Reconsider an example presented earlier. I am bored by a particular conversation. Now there are various ways in which this experience of boredom might be explained. In one imagined scenario, I could be bored because I am deaf or hard of hearing and so unable to access much of the information to which I am exposed. The conversation is experienced either as being shrouded in silence (although there may be visual cues that suggest its content) or as a buzz of noise. In either case, I may become frustrated, feel trapped in the situation, and grow bored.

In another imagined instance, I am perfectly able to hear the sounds of people conversing, but I am unable to hear it as something meaningful because I do not understand the language in which the conversation is being conducted. I may comprehend some words or phrases, make interpretive inferences based on inflection or tone of voice, but the conversation as a whole is relatively meaningless to me. Boredom is not altogether inevitable in such an instance (boredom is never inevitable). I could attend to and amuse myself with alternative stimuli embedded in the situation. I could imaginatively construe the conversation as being about this or that fascinating topic—literally, pretend that it is interesting. Or I could sustain interest in the conversation because of my admittedly vague knowledge of its content or because of the way that it has been framed, even though I am unable to understand the words. (It might take the form of a foreign news commentary on some episode that I know to be of enormous significance, or an exchange between judge and jury announcing a life or death verdict on someone whom I love.) Or I could simply become bored.

But suppose that my hearing is in no way impaired and that the conversants are speaking in a language in which I am fluent. Moreover, assume that the speakers are plainly audible and that there is no excess of distracting noise in the environment. Still, I am bored. Now what sense does it make to portray this latter experience of boredom as a consequence of "semiotic breakdown"?

It might seem to make very little sense, perhaps, if the conversation is one that virtually any listener would judge to be deadly dull, apparently without wit or purpose, seemingly devoid of meaningful content. Here I would have failed to interpret the conversation as interesting, but "failed to" in the limited sense of "did not," rather than the more negative sense of "could not" or "should have but did not."

Nevertheless, it would be a mistake to conclude that talk about failure here makes no sense at all. Someone else might take great interest in the conversation, and for any variety of reasons. The "majority judgment" that the conversation is dull, devoid of meaning, remains a judgment; that is to say, an interpretation. The form in which this judgment is expressed can mislead one to embrace the conclusion that the conversation is "intrinsically" boring or meaningless. Yet from the very beginning of my inquiry I have rejected that sort of conclusion. "Boredom" and "meaning" are concepts that describe a relationship—a person's semiotic relationship to some situation, thing, or activity. What is boring to one person can be of great interest to another.[2] Their different experiences represent different interpretations.

This is true, I would contend, even in the case of two persons who appear to have equal access to the very same information. So they both can hear the conversation; they both are fluent in the language; they both understand the subject matter of the conversation, and so forth. Yet one finds it boring and the other does not. Here, equal access to information does not entail that for both individuals the experience will be equally meaningful. In this case, their feeling responses to what they hear are different. Since I want to argue, following Peirce, that these feelings are part of what the experience means to them, it makes sense to say that they interpret the conversation differently, and that one of them fails to find it interesting.[3]

The judgment that this failure is of little or great consequence has always, of course, to be made by somebody. Disagreements about such judgments can fuel controversy, in the aesthetic realm as well as in the ethical. This does not always happen. With regard to judgments of taste, a conflict of interpretations might be perceived by some persons as tolerable, even desirable. (Why should everyone else have to share my experience of X as beautiful?) Even in the case of moral judgments, it is widely assumed that cultural, individual, and situational differences can dramatically shape the manner in which persons "see" things, and evaluate them. Yet frequently enough the differences are not tolerated, so that, for example, a mountain vista will be regarded by people as so beautiful, a suffering infant so clearly deserving of care and nurture, that they conclude there must be something wrong with someone who fails to perceive these facts, who is "insensitive" to them.

In various religious traditions, persons who fail to perceive the religious significance of things, to take delight in spiritual goods, to sustain interest in religious practices, and so forth are often judged to have "something wrong" with them. This incapacity might be described as a kind of spiritual "blindness," or it can be more akin to a lack of skill, the lack of a certain power of discernment that can be practiced and developed. It might be attributed to a weakness of will, especially insofar as the will guides and fixes attention. And it is sometimes portrayed as a jaded insensitivity, a "hardness of heart" that precludes powerful religious emotion as well as insight.

I am not suggesting either that these various forms of religious incapacity are perfectly distinct from one another or that no important differences exist among them. The characteristic feature that they share, the common element that I want to expose here, is the one that makes them all relevant to my semiotic deliberations. However else one might choose to characterize them, it is safe to say these incapacities have the pragmatic consequence of making religiously meaningful interpretations problematic. A person thus incapacitated will find it difficult or even impossible, in his ongoing, everyday experience of the world, to discern the religious significance of things (as it is posited and evaluated in various ways by different religious communities). Moreover, in specific situations or activities (for example, prayer, meditation, worship, ritual performances) where others are engaged, involved, attentive, joyful, bound to one another by feelings of powerful *communitas*, such a person is alienated, fidgety, distracted . . . bored.

Talk about "incapacities" makes it seem as if these, too, are somehow completely intrinsic to individuals. But since semiosis is a relationship between an inter-

141

preter and some object of interpretation, semiotic incapacities must also be analyzed in relational terms. I
may fail to see you across the room because of my poor
vision or because my eyes are closed or because the
lighting is poor or I am distracted or you are hidden
from view. In each case, one can speak of semiotic
breakdown, a disrupted flow of information. Yet the
causal factor, the "incapacitating" factor, in each case
is quite different.

Every effect is a sign of its cause. That is why boredom is itself a sign requiring interpretation. Just as the
potential causes of semiotic breakdown are multiple,
so can the boredom that might result from this state of
affairs be explained in multiple ways. At various points
in this discussion, I have referred to the sorts of traditional explanations that religious communities supply
for spiritual boredom. Slothfulness, weakness of will,
neglect of devotion are all possible candidates. So are
fatigue, illness, or the temptation posed by excessive
distractions. Even the divine reality can be posited as
an explanation, its transcendent or mysterious nature
causing it to be "hidden" from ordinary human perceptions. In some theistic traditions, this "hiding" is regarded as intentional on the part of the Deity, executed
as a "test" of human patience and devotion.

Clearly, then, the interpretation of boredom as a sign
is also a task that requires skill, discernment, maybe
even practice. Moreover, no meaningful interpretation
is likely to be possible if this sign is ignored or not taken
seriously. That was Pascal's warning; also Heidegger's.

142

Recall how John of the Cross and Aquinas both remarked that one crucial factor distinguishing the inevitable experience of spiritual dryness from the sin of acedia is the fact that a person will be troubled by the former, will very much care about his boredom. So in a remarkable way, what I do about my boredom, the manner in which I respond to it, is part of the interpretation of what that boredom means, and may even be a clue to its cause.[4] But I cannot respond to boredom if I do not pay attention to it or take it seriously. That is a point rather consistently made by the saints and sages whose advice I have surveyed here. And it is that advice, more than anything else, that motivated this inquiry.

SEMIOSIS IS an interpretive process that involves the continuous production of new signs, each itself subject to further interpretation. Human experience, from the simplest sensations and emotions to the most complex judgments about states of affairs, takes the form of semiosis. These are Peirce's insights, presupposed rather than defended here. My interest is in extending these insights, by applying them to the consideration of boredom as a special kind or quality of experience.

Boredom, as a response to anything, constitutes at least a part of the interpretation of that thing. At the same time, boredom is a sign open to interpretation. In its most profound form, however, boredom is not a response to any particular thing—is not a being bored with this or that. It is dispositional, pervasive. What, then, does this boredom interpret? If it is to be regarded as a sign, what might it signify? (Something about the self, perhaps, but this something is nothing, the "self as nought.")[5]

Since it is not linked or determined as a response to any particular thing, in a peculiar sense, it is a response to no (particular) thing. I want to suggest, then, that such a boredom is an interpretation of nothing, signifies nothing, but that (for reasons already indicated) this nothing matters. Nothingness cannot be imagined, so that in the attempted contemplation of it, the imagination fails. From a religious point of view, this failure can be productive (if it purifies love, inspires detachment) or disastrous (if it eventuates in chronic boredom and despair). These possibilities differ dramatically; but I have tried to argue that they share a certain logic. That logic can also be described in semiotic terms (as Peirce himself was more than blithe to do).

Now it is the interdependence of induction and abduction in Peirce's theory of inquiry, I suspect, that may provide further insight into the relationship between boredom and the religious imagination. Recall that the concept of habit was central to Peirce's account. Indeed, habits play a key role in the abductive reasoning of Musement, continuously shaping and informing the Muser's cognitive activity. Abduction generates hypotheses that can then be inductively tested; but induction produces habits of thought.[6] These function within abductive inferences as premises or "leading principles," whether they be conscious or unconscious, explicitly formulated or implicit and unarticulated.

Cognitive habits typically take the form of beliefs. A

144

belief about X will function as a habit generating all sorts of expectations about how X will behave under certain circumstances, what qualities it will tend to display, what relationships it will be likely to establish, and so on. To have no beliefs or habits of thought at all is virtually to be incapable of cognition. On the other hand, the person who is equipped with the right sorts of habits is a cognitively skilled individual capable of great creativity.

Some of these habits are empirical beliefs about things. They allow me to perceive, in particular cases, that a thing encountered is of this or that kind, to recognize it as such. At the same time, Musement is also sustained by a habit of play that requires me to have all such beliefs "as though I did not have them." Therein lies the creative power of abductive reasoning, not only in the application of class concepts to things observed (even in the most routine sort of abduction this already involves an imaginative "leap"), but in the experimental mixing and matching of concepts and beliefs, their reformulation and reconfiguration, combined with a readiness to let this process be shaped by whatever presents itself in experience. This readiness manifests itself as a certain indifference. It is an indifference-as-playfulness, a genuine receptivity or openness to how and what things are (not merely "in themselves" but as they shape our interpretations).

For Peirce, abduction was also the mode of reasoning involved in recognizing the "essence" of a thing.[7] Once again, general beliefs about kinds of things are formed inductively, but to perceive any particular X as being this or that sort of thing, that is, to recognize *X* as a *Y*, is to reason abductively. In Peirce's view, the essence of a thing is the "final cause" that lends it its intelligibility and determines its natural behavior. Reasoning from effect (as a sign) to cause is always an instance of abduction, in this case, proceeding from an observation of the manifest behavior of a thing to its essential nature.

This helps to explain why Peirce understood Musement to be a meditative exercise of potentially religious significance. His general perspective on these matters was shared by the Jesuit poet Gerard Manley Hopkins. Hopkins (Ignatian in his general outlook but, like Peirce, very much influenced by Duns Scotus's metaphysics) correlated his notion of "inscape" with the essential or inward "nature" of a thing.[8] Much of Hopkins's poetic musing was devoted to the contemplation of such inscapes (the "more" in experience), especially as they can be discerned in the world of nature. Conceived as natural kinds rather than simply as convenient human classifications, he believed them to signify the divine presence of their Creator. For Peirce too, the world was God's "great poem," embodying symbols of the divine purpose.[9] These signs are most readily interpreted by the individual who engages in Musement, not as a sporadic exercise, but as a regular practice.

How are these considerations relevant to my characterization of boredom as a semiotic phenomenon? Sign-interpretation is an abductive process. It involves the hypothesizing of "explanations" for particular signs and symbols, by contemplating these signs and playing with their potential meanings or patterns of meaning. Such play can be quite enjoyable (as it often is when mediated by a work of art) and can produce great insight. But how, to reframe my question, is the experience of boredom relevant to this sort of play and to this kind of insight?

Redundancy may help to precipitate boredom; but it is also the life-blood of induction. Inductive inferences form habits of thought because of the regularities and redundancies in the experiences that ground these inferences. Moreover, abduction is permeated by such habits, presupposes them, and yields insight as a result of them. The belief that a certain kind of thing will manifest specific characteristics predisposes one, when one happens to perceive just this configuration of characteristics in X, to classify X as a thing of that kind. Of course, a surprising or transformative experience, for example, one's encounter with a powerful work of art, may challenge one's beliefs and habits of thought, and suggest new classifications. Nevertheless, a person engages in aesthetic play already equipped with an immense variety of such habits formed by his or her everyday experience of the world. Art both utilizes and transforms this experience. It is not a mere negation, but truly a "transfiguration of the commonplace."[10] So the creative imagination finds in the boredom of everydayness not merely the stimulus of "repulsion" (Kierkegaard's observation), but rather, some of its own "leading principles," the rules by which it plays.

Habit may be regarded as one of the causes of boredom, then, insofar as it constitutes the terminus of an activity, for example, the result or consequence of inductive

147

reasoning. But insofar as it is a premise or presupposition, the creative source of a thinking process, it is to be regarded as a skill facilitating insight. Of course, a nondeductive inferential process is not bound by any law of necessity to yield specific results. Habits of thought are formed inductively, but no induction can be guaranteed to establish a particular habit or, indeed, any habit at all. (Two individuals sampling the same data may form different conclusions or be unable to articulate any generalizable result.) Similarly, the mere possession of specific beliefs or thought-habits does not determine in advance what sort of hypothetical insight the person possessing them will arrive at or, once again, whether she will achieve any insight at all. In the latter instance, when no insight dawns, one experiences a kind of semiotic breakdown. A sign is perceived for which no meaning can be discerned or its character as a sign may not even be recognized. In the persistent absence of meaning, boredom creeps in and finds a home.

Here boredom is the consequence of a lack of interpretive skill, an inability to process certain types of information. In other instances, boredom results because such skill is so well developed that its exercise has become trivial. Paradoxically, however, an increase in interpretive skill can produce the sudden awareness of the existence of new information, sometimes a completely different type of information, or a new relationship among bits of information already perceived. It has been previously observed how when any activity becomes habitual, one no longer needs constantly and consciously to attend to it, and thus one may grow bored. At the same time, one becomes free to attend to other dimensions or aspects of the activity or situation.

Note carefully that this freedom does not take the form of a license to ignore something altogether in the search for variety, new stimuli. Wandering of attention is one of the symptoms of a distracted state of mind. The bored consciousness may yield to distraction, of course, but it might also be disposed to refocus attention on things now perceived as boring. Indeed, it is a peculiar fact about boredom that it sometimes moves a person to notice the aspects of things or the features of experience that are typically cloaked in everydayness, taken for granted, regarded as insignificant. (Not being presently occupied or otherwise engaged, the bored person is suddenly free to notice this or that, to see things in a different way.)

Now everything that enters into experience is potentially a sign, and every sign is multivalent, with a potentially infinite set of meanings. The sign is present but its object is absent, something referred to, not presented but represented. It is the something "*more* to experience and *more in* what we experience than we can predict." Boredom is a sign of this absence; but equally, at least potentially, it is a sign of this something "more" revealed at the very heart of things, a greater depth of meaning.

For example, having become bored with all of the useful things that I can do with a given tool or device, I may suddenly begin to contemplate its aesthetic qualities. Bored with the conversation at a party or meeting,

149

I may find myself playfully enthralled with people's voices and with the sounds of their accents. No longer interested in carefully observing an object for some specific purpose, I may suddenly begin to "see" it in a new light. And having become bored with someone that I love, I may discover myself falling in love with that person all over again, but not simply "again," because here something new has been added to that love and to the relationship. Moreover, that "something" will have been discovered, not in the restless search for a new beloved, but right here in this place, the same place where love had grown weary, now suddenly reborn.

Such a birth of fresh insight may seem like a purely spontaneous, even serendipitous occurrence to the person who experiences it. Nevertheless, Peirce was convinced that it could be described in logical categories, while not rigidly determined, that such occurrences were governed by a general law: "Logical analysis applied to mental phenomena shows that there is but one law of mind, namely, that ideas tend to spread continuously and to affect certain others which stand to them in a peculiar relation of affectibility. In this spreading they lose intensity, and especially the power of affecting others, but gain generality and become welded with other ideas."[11]

The experience of boredom is the experience of just such a loss of "intensity," a fact that Peirce himself observed and one that he explicated in terms of the dulling power of habits of expectation.[12] This loss is compensated for, however, by a commensurate gain in "generality." Generality, the welding of ideas one to another, the coordination of ideas, is precisely what is involved, on Peirce's account, in the acquisition of any skill, including the skill required for abductive reasoning. Consequently, insofar it takes the form of such a loss of intensity, boredom should be regarded both as inevitable and as having a positive role to play in the development of mind and the growth of human knowledge.

> Habit is that specialisation of the law of mind whereby a general idea gains the power of exciting reactions. But in order that the general idea should attain all its functionality, it is necessary, also, that it should become suggestible by sensations. That is accomplished by a psychical process having the form of a hypothetic inference. . . . Now the mind acts in a way similar to this, every time we acquire a power of coordinating reactions in a peculiar way, as in performing any act requiring skill. . . . The same mental process is many times employed whenever we are learning to speak a language or are acquiring any sort of skill.[13]

Habit is skill that displays itself as a certain "power of exciting reactions." That power is harnessed and that skill is exercised in every abductive inference whereby a general idea becomes "suggestible by sensations," linked as a rule to some case. What results is significance, the birth of meaning as a semiotic event. This birth can also be experienced as a "gift" of meaning (William James's contention) for all of the reasons that abductive inferences have been described as indeterminate. That is, in the event that another, different thought-habit had been engaged, a different rule applied to this particular case, the result would have differed. Moreover, the force of any given habit is itself "gentle," determining no specific result but only one of a certain general character. Recall that this indeterminacy characterizes ordinary sense perceptions as well as the most complex and elaborate cogitations.

All perceptual judgments have been identified as abductions. In fact, every sensation is a predicate that "fulfills the function of an hypothesis"[14] (expressible, in simplest terms, by utterances like "this is green" or "this is loud" or "this is beautiful" or "this is painful"). Feelings and sensations, like conceptions (indeed, *as* vague conceptions) are never immediate or unmediated, but are always determined by some previous cognition. On this account, human consciousness is a continuous stream of semiosis, each cognition determined by others and so functioning as a *sign* of those others. Feelings and emotions, of course, may seem to us to have a quality of immediacy, to arise spontaneously.

> But there is no feeling which is not also a representation, a predicate of something determined logically by the feelings which precede it. For if there are any such feelings not predicates, they are the emotions. Now every emotion has a subject. If a man is angry, he is saying to himself that this or that is vile or outrageous. If he is in joy, he is saying "this is delicious." If he is wondering, he is saying "this is strange." In short, whenever a man feels, he is thinking of *something*.[15]

Peirce concluded his argument with the observation that "even those passions which have no definite object

—as melancholy—only come to consciousness by tinging the *objects of thought.*" Notice that joy could
have served Peirce as an example here just as well as
melancholy, not the specific sort of enjoyment that is
expressed by "this is delicious," but a deeper, abiding
joy that has "no definite object" (something akin to
Ignatius's "consolation without a cause"). In the same
way, boredom would work as an example (recall the
earlier portrayal of ennui as a boredom that shades into
melancholy). This would not be the kind of boredom
that moves one to say "this is boring", but the more
profound sense (to invoke Heidegger once again) in
which "I, myself, am bored" or "it is boring for one";
such a boredom "radiates out" over things.

Whatever form they might take, the pertinent fact
remains that all of these feelings are predicates that
fulfill the (interpretive) function of hypotheses. They
might be attached to particular objects of experience or
they might have no definite object. In the latter case,
being predicated of no (particular) thing they become
predicable of any and every thing, "tinging the objects
of thought." It is in this sense that the deepest form of
boredom is an interpretation of nothing, but this nothingness often seems to pervade all things, infecting the
various objects of experience, coloring them with gray-
ness, drawing them into a fog.

MEDITATION IS the exercise of attention. What one
chooses to pay attention to, for any particular purpose,
can prove to be of enormous significance. But it is a significant fact in itself that attention is something that

must be exercised or practiced. It is not intuitively clear that this should be the case. Paying attention might seem to some persons to be a relatively straightforward thing to do. One attends to X or one does not, like turning a flashlight on or off. Assuming the absence of tremendous distraction, this is not something that would appear necessarily to require a great deal of skill.

The assumption about distraction is not an innocent one. Even in a sense deprivation chamber, the human imagination is a fertile source of infinitely numerous possible distractions. In point of fact, the evidence suggests that individuals forced to endure such a "low information" environment for any duration of time are vulnerable to states of high distraction, even hallucination. I am convinced that such evidence lends empirical substance to Pascal's suspicion that "the sole cause of man's unhappiness is that he does not know how to stay quietly in his room."[16] But to pursue the analysis of this evidence would surely constitute a distraction from my immediate concern, prevent me from attending to attention.

What, then, does it mean to exercise attention? Consider, first, what it means to "exercise" anything at all. (This may be a distraction well worth pursuing!)

"Exercise," in the most basic and also the vaguest sense of the word, is an "act of bringing into play."[17] Such an act presupposes some sort of power or capability. Of course, it is true of any action that in order to perform it one must have the power to act or be capable of so acting. What distinguishes exercise from other forms of activity is that its very purpose is the bringing of such powers or capabilities "into play." Admittedly, this distinction is not absolute. Since any given activity can have multiple purposes, it is possible to exercise while doing something else. Moreover, and for the very same reason, it is possible to regard the doing of anything at all as a form of exercise. I may vote in order to get my candidate elected, but at the same time I exercise my right, my power to vote. I may walk each morning to the corner store in order to purchase a newspaper, but my walking is also an exercising of those various and complex physical capabilities required for ambulation. In both cases, on can recognize examples of an activity that might fall under a variety of descriptions. Those descriptions that focus on the agent's faculties, skills or powers, insofar as these are engaged or employed in the activity, construe it primarily as exercise.

Neither of these examples is paradigmatic for my discussion of exercising attention, because neither displays very clearly the particular features of an exercise that would dispose one to regard it as a type of training or *practice*. To think of exercise as practice is to identify as the purpose of such activity not merely the "bringing into play" of some otherwise dormant power or skill, but also, the augmentation of the latter as a direct consequence of the activity. This is play with a purpose, but not just any purpose; the purpose here is not political, for example, nor does it involve the making of a purchase, etc. Practice is a self-reflexive and a self-transforming activity. Any specific activity may have many different consequences, but in the case of practice, the relevant consequence is the exercising and perfecting of a skill. One practices in order to get better at the doing of something. Whatever effects upon various *objects* an exercise might produce, the significant results of practice involve changes wrought within a *subject*, the practitioner or exercitant.

Peirce conceived of Musement as just such a practice, as "a lively exercise of one's powers." Although "not as commonly practiced as it ought to be," he promised that if even as little as "five to six percent of one's waking time" were invested in this exercise, the results would more than "repay the expenditure."[18] Musement was portrayed as a form of meditative thinking that, over a period of time, would likely "flower" into religious awareness. Such insight or awareness was not to be regarded either as an immediate or an automatic consequence of the activity. In fact, Peirce cautioned against regarding it even as the principal objective of Musement. Rather, the primary purpose of this activity is exercise, more specifically, the practice of attention and observation, the lively engagement of one's imagination and powers of reasoning, and the bringing into play of various affections, feeling responses to the objects of contemplation.

First and foremost, however, Musement is the exercise of attention. It begins with "attentive observation," the "drinking in" of sense impressions. It must be practiced "with your eyes open, awake to what is about or within you." Even though it may begin with the sort of attention that one pays to any object of careful observation, Musement must evolve into the more fully engaged and lively attentiveness displayed by someone who is engrossed in "conversation" with another sub-ject or self. "Open your eyes," Peirce counseled, "and your heart, which also is a perceptive organ."[19] These are the necessary qualities prescribed for Musement, that it must be a disinterested practice of attention, pursued with "open heart."

Nearly half a century earlier, Peirce had recorded some important observations about the nature of atten-tion, in the very same series of essays that embodied his first detailed account of human cognition as semiosis.[20] Attention is the "power of abstraction." he explained, by means of which "emphasis is put upon one of the objective elements of consciousness." It is a fundamen-tal ingredient of thought, in particular, of inductive thinking, and thus it plays a decisive role in habit for-mation.

> Attention is roused when the same phenomenon presents itself repeatedly on different occasions, or the same predi-cate in different subjects. We see that A has a certain char-acter, that B has the same, C has the same; and this excites our attention, so that we say "*These* have this character." Thus attention is an act of induction. . . .
>
> Attention produces effects upon the nervous system. These effects are habits, or nervous associations. A habit arises, when, having had the sensation of performing a cer-tain act, *m*, on several occasions *a, b, c*, we come to do it upon every occurrence of the general event, *l*, of which *a, b* and *c* are special cases. . . .
>
> Thus the formation of habit is an induction, and is nec-essarily connected with attention or abstraction.[21]

Notice how this description of attention identifies it (much like awakening) as neither a purely active nor a passive phenomenon. Guided by the will, it is an active power of abstracting or emphasizing one or another element of consciousness. At the same time, attention is "roused" or "excited" by sensations, by continuities or similarities among phenomena. Consider, again, the interdependence of abduction and induction, not just as complementary stages in some elaborate theoretical inquiry, but as interwoven strands of inference that shape our everyday experience of the world.

> Everything in which we take the least interest creates in us its own particular emotion, however slight this may be. This emotion is a sign and a predicate of the thing. Now, when a thing resembling this thing is presented to us, a similar emotion arises; hence, we immediately infer that the former is like the latter.[22]

The attaching of any sensation, emotion or conception to something as a predicate, as an interpretive sign of that thing, is abduction. Inductively, habits are established in consciousness, generating the expectation that different things bearing the same predicate will be of the same or similar kind; they are perceived as cases governed by the same general rule. The practice of attention is an active process, then, but not an arbitrary one. It is responsive to and shaped by the continuities among phenomena, aroused by or receptive to (more or less) the way that things appear.[23] Insofar as patterns of meaning emerge in experience at all, however, it is, in part, because of acquired habits formed by acts of attention. (I say "in part" because Peirce believed some of these patterns to be generated by innate dispositions or natural "instincts.")[24] Consequently, it is no contradiction to insist that, within such experience, meaning is both created and discovered. From this Peircean point of view, meaning will have the character of an "event" —one that establishes a semiotic relationship between interpreting subject and signified object.

In short, the practice of paying attention is a process of habit formation, and habit is skill.[25] This is true, despite the fact that habit may also have a "stultifying" effect, resulting in a "loss of intensity" of consciousness. Here, temporary boredom is the price that one might have to pay for the development of habits of feeling, thought, and action. These habits are the rules governing imaginative play, the premises shaping abductive inferences; as such, they make meaning possible.

In what sense, though, must the Muser's practice of attention be disinterested or (in Peirce's terminology) "purposeless"? I can attend to a thing for a great many specific purposes, whether that thing be an object, a tool, an idea, a feeling, or some other person. Each specific purpose will itself generate habits of expectation, determining in advance what features of the thing my attention will tend to abstract or emphasize, how it will be perceived. In contrast, the disinterested observer is attentive, but to no determinate, preselected aspect of a thing, thus remaining open ("awake") to whatever appears.

Now I want to suggest that this particular way of paying attention, in itself, requires practice—the development over time of a certain habit of detachment, the repeated cultivation of that habit. This sort of practice, it seems to me, would require that one be attentive to the manner in which one pays attention . . . not just any kind of paying attention will be suitable for meditation.[26]

Even though religious insight is not designated as the explicit goal or purpose of Musement, Peirce regarded such insight as a likely consequence of the Muser's activity. This is the case because the skills that are sharpened in meditative thinking are the very type that are well adapted to religious knowing. In other writings, Peirce made this point more straightforwardly. If, he once suggested, as much time were spent in prayer as we devote to social interactions of various kinds, our knowledge of God would be as firm as that which we possess regarding human companions. The basic problem is that our religious exercises are "sporadic, not incessant";[27] and so the sort of information relevant to discerning religious meaning is not easily processed.

The context for this suggestion makes it clear that the "prayer" Peirce was recommending little resembles formal petitionary or liturgical prayer, but is much more like the free, open, purposeless communing with the divine mind that he was later to describe as Musement. Indeed, it was through such meditation upon the "physico-psychical universe" (God's "great poem") that history's most prominent religious sages (Peirce mentioned the Buddha, Confucius, and Socrates) were imbued with powerful habits of feeling, thought, and conduct, enabling them to perceive fragments of the divine nature. For them it was all a matter of paying attention to the universe, and of paying attention in a distinctive way.

I have proposed that the logic of Ignatius of Loyola's spiritual exercises is also abductive, something akin to Musement. With Ignatius, the subject matter for meditation was carefully defined as religious; its purpose was also designated as such. Nevertheless, Ignatius's method was experimental (as Rahner observed), in much the same way as Peirce's. Whatever the precise matter of the meditation, the exercitant was to be ready for anything that might occur, indifferent toward particular results, desiring only to know and to do the will of God.

The apparent contrast with Peirce, at least to some extent then, is misleading. To be sure, Ignatius was far less reluctant than Peirce to identify the purpose of these exercises. As he stipulated it, that purpose was twofold: first, "the disposing of the soul to rid itself of all inordinate attachments," and second, "the seeking and finding the will of God in the disposition of our life."[28] Note the self-reflexive character of these exercises, the focus on dispositional changes wrought within the exercitant. Note, further, the precise nature of the dispositions that are being exercised and developed: the first, a certain habit of detachment; the second, a power of discerning how the will of God is manifested in one's life. As Ignatius's remarks make clear, the one is a presupposition of the other. The explicitly religious purpose is achieved only on the presupposition of indifference. In semiotic terms, interpretive skill, of the sort that enables a person to discern the divine will operative in everyday occurrences, requires for its own proper exercise a certain attitude of detachment. The individual who has developed such an attitude as habitual is best equipped to read the signs embedded in human experience as religiously meaningful.

As a consequence, the exercitant must pay attention to those signs while at the same time paying attention to the way in which attention is paid. This is less confusing, I hope, than it appeared at first glance, since *how* one pays attention (with indifference or with selfish interest) is itself a sign, potentially revelatory. Moreover, *whatever* one experiences (e.g., consolation or desolation) *whenever* one pays attention (to one's own sinfulness, or an episode in the life of Christ, or some imagined scenario, as in Ignatius's meditation on the "Two Standards") is also a religiously meaningful sign. That is part of the rationale for Ignatius's listing of interpretive "rules" for the discernment of spirits.

The spiritual exercises enact a process of semiosis that is complex and multilayered. The exercitant must pay attention to various symbols, stories, images, and ideas. Themselves multivalent, these serve to evoke in the exercitant thoughts, feelings, and motivations to action that are equally sign-like in character and loaded with potential meaning. Every interpretation is a sign, subject to further interpretation. And Ignatius, no less than Peirce, conceived of sensations and feeling responses (in addition to conceptions) both as interpretations and as interpretable. (Most relevant to my inquiry are the feelings of joy or joylessness that can arise in meditation, even as they shape its progress.)

This last point of agreement between Peirce and Ignatius touches on a matter of vital importance. On neither account is meditation to be regarded purely as an intellectual exercise. Attention in meditation is not to be focused exclusively or even primarily on abstract concepts. Musement fully engages the senses, emotions, and the imagination; it culminates in a powerful sensation of beauty, "stirring" the heart of the Muser to adoration and the love of God.[29] Likewise, Ignatius's method of meditation is distinguished by the extent to which it encourages the imaginative "application of the senses" to the various objects of meditation.[30] One of the purposes of such an exercise is its efficacy in arousing strong emotions, feelings that not only have great interpretive value, but also can move the heart to greater love, to more perfect adoration.

Introducing insights gleaned from the writings of Jonathan Edwards at the conclusion of my reflections may seem to represent an inexcusable distraction (especially since I intend only to indicate those insights without exploring them in any detail).[31] But there are striking similarities of opinion among Edwards, Peirce, and Ignatius (three thinkers otherwise so pronouncedly different in background and perspective) on certain topics related to this inquiry. In his *Treatise Concerning Religious Affections*, Edwards, much like Ignatius in the formulation of his "rules," offered guidelines for the proper interpretation of various types of religious experience. Ingredients of such experience, like those feelings of consolation and desolation in Ignatius, like the various feelings that are aroused in Musement for Peirce, have the quality of a *sign*.

Edwards identified twelve signs that are especially important within his interpretive scheme as indicating a genuine experience of the divine reality. Included in his lengthy explication and analysis of those signs are three observations that I want to underscore for their relevance to my theme. First is Edwards's contention that true religious experience will often involve a sensible delight in the divine presence. This delight is caused by a powerful sensation of the divine beauty as it is radiantly visible to the interpreter of the "book of nature" (the latter being a metaphor for the whole of creation conceived as divine semiosis). Second is his insistence that the love inspired by this beauty must be a truly disinterested love, in much the same way that Kant insisted on disinterestedness for genuine aesthetic experience, and Ignatius on *indiferencia* for the true love of God.

Finally, Edwards argued that chief among all the signs of God's grace is Christian "practice," a practice that signifies the presence of gracious affections in the soul even as it represents their proper "exercise." This emphasis on practice is evidence that Edwards's interpretive method was also thoroughly "experimental." It is most certainly a method that was solidly grounded in inductive reasoning. Edwards was not particularly impressed by the significance of isolated moods or flashes of feeling. Holy affections, rather, are discernible patterns or habits of feeling that help to shape a person's thinking and behavior in the long run.

"Christian practice" was a complex category for Edwards, embracing but not limited to certain "immanent acts" of the soul, such as prayerful contemplation. Indeed, the habits exercised in contemplation were expected to bear fruit in outward and observable acts of faithfulness, of courageous sacrifice, and of love. "Ye shall know them by their fruits" is a biblical maxim that Edwards perceived as the chief rule for the discernment of spirits, even as Peirce regarded it as an earlier version of his own pragmatic maxim.[32] As with Peirce, for Edwards human conduct was best understood as a form of semiosis. "There is a language in actions," he observed, "and in some cases, much more clear and convincing than in words."[33] Consequently, every action is potentially an act of interpretation, and itself a sign whose meaning is open to further determination. Habits of thought and feeling can be displayed in action; and the meaning of an experience will frequently be expressed there.

The trials endured in Christian practice mark it both as the most reliable sign and as the "proper *experiment* of the truth and power of our godliness."[34] Edwards considered such trials to be "the balances in which our hearts are weighed."[35] This balance metaphor, like Ignatius's, is designed to reveal something about the love of God as an ideal for the religious aspirant. Though in a way quite different from Ignatius's "balance at equilibrium," it also exposes the special quality of indifference that is required for such a love.

165

I have tried in these pages to portray boredom as a sign. It is a sign that can be interpreted in various ways, sometimes as a sign of sin, a sign of failure. It can be a sign of fatigue, a healthy sign marking as trivial those objects on which we ought not wastefully to spend our attention. Boredom can also be interpreted as a trial, in its deepest and darkest manifestations, as a terrible trial of our love, so that it, too, becomes like a balance "in which our hearts are weighed."

POSTLUDE

ON WAITING

> To detach our desire from all good things and to
> wait. Experience proves that this waiting is satisfied.
> It is then we touch the absolute good.
> — SIMONE WEIL

WAITING CAN be boring.[1]
Waiting for a long time can be very boring. Nevertheless, the spiritual practices of a great variety of religious
traditions involve waiting, indeed, sometimes can be
perceived as consisting essentially in acts of waiting.
If boredom is capable of defeating these practices, then
it ought to be taken seriously, not only by the devotee
who engages in such disciplines, but by the philosopher
engaged in trying to understand them. That is another
one of the reasons why I wrote this book.

Waiting, like boredom, is itself a complex phenomenon that merits careful scrutiny. I can wait for some-

one or something with a clear conception of what I am waiting for, and a relatively clear sense of how long it will take for my expectations to be fulfilled. Knowledge is power, in some instances the power to control. The knowledge of who/what I am waiting for and how long I must endure the waiting implies some degree of control, on my part, over this state of affairs. If I am an employer about to interview a candidate for an important position, then I probably already have a significant amount of information (in the form of a curriculum vitae, letters of recommendation, and so on) about this person, and I can be reasonably confident that he or she will arrive for the meeting on time. But this is not the sort of control that I can expect to exercise over my spiritual life.

Prepositions make a difference in how we understand the phenomenon of waiting. I can wait *for* someone or something, and I can do so for a great many imaginable reasons. I can also wait *on* someone, and here waiting implies service, like that supplied by a store clerk to a customer, or a vassal to a king. This can be a formal political or economic relationship. It can also be a loving service; whether or not they would want to describe it as such, parents often wait on their children, and sometimes the reverse is true as well. Waiting on someone involves being responsive to their needs, desires, or wishes. This is the sort of service that Jesus recommended to his disciples as a paradigm for the religious life.

Now waiting *on* someone could obviously require me to wait *for* that person (or for something needed or desired by that person) under certain circumstances. Indeed, "waiting for," I want to suggest, implies the more basic understanding of what it means to wait, with "waiting on" invoking a derivative sense of the word. Nor should all forms of "waiting on" be taken as the embodiment of a religious ideal; that is to say, waiting on someone might take the form of a mutually destructive or spiritually unhealthy relationship, as in examples like prostitution or slavery.

Waiting might appear to be the sort of thing that either one is prepared or not to do. If one chooses to do it, then the waiting itself seems relatively straightforward, easy to accomplish. On the contrary, I want to argue that waiting, in the spiritually significant sense, can constitute a formidable task; it takes practice. When Hesse's Siddhartha announces that he can think, he can fast, and he can wait, he is identifying impressive credentials, abilities that he took great pains to develop.[2] On the other hand, waiting is not something that Jesus' disciples were *able* to do. Their behavior in Gethsemane represents a failure rather than a refusal to wait, as even Jesus recognized with his judgment that "the spirit is willing."

In a contemporary culture organized around fast food, sound bites, and virtually immediate access to information, waiting can be perceived as a sign of weakness or lack of expertise; thus, the capacity required for waiting may never be developed at all. Moreover, waiting is often eschewed because it can signify a relationship in which the distribution of power is asymmetrical: the poor wait on the wealthy who can afford to employ

169

their services; important people should not be left waiting; physicians may eventually serve their patients, but it is the patients who sit in "waiting rooms." What distinguishes this contemporary, negative perspective on waiting from the perspective of Jesus or from Siddhartha's point of view? Waiting, like boredom, would appear to be a complex sign, interpretable in a variety of ways.

"For" and "on" are both prepositions that take an object. When the object and the length of my waiting are indeterminate, the act of waiting is itself dramatically transformed. That is to say, when I have no sense of what I am waiting for or how long I must be prepared to wait, then I am engaged in an act of waiting pure and simple. Not a waiting for this or that; rather, I *myself* am waiting. What is manifested here is a dispositional property of the one who waits, not a discrete act but a fundamental way of being. Waiting as a spiritual exercise seems typically to take this latter form. "Take heed, watch; for you do not know when the time will come."[3]

Waiting of this kind is a supreme exercise of attention. I can wait for my friend in a restaurant while reading a newspaper. I know for whom I am waiting and approximately when he will arrive. But if I am waiting for a stranger and the time of arrival is uncertain, then I must pay continuous attention to what is happening, and to whomever appears. This attention will take the form of a looking for signs that the person I am waiting for has arrived. So it is simultaneously an exercise in interpretation. Finally, if I pay exclusive attention to one door of the restaurant, the person for whom I am waiting may come in through another entrance unnoticed. This means that my waiting must also involve the practice of detachment.

For many of the reasons that waiting is an important religious skill, it is also crucial to the success of scientific inquiry, of the experimental method. A scientist who is impatient to get just the results that she is hoping for will very likely distort the actual data, drawing false inferences. Peirce understood this and that is why so much of his argument for the reality of God was devoted to a discussion of proper scientific method.

Any act of interpretation is a complex act of attention. It involves attending to both something present and something represented, a sign and its object. The sign may be visible, accessible, tangible—in most respects, determinate. But the sign's object may be absent, even as its meaning may be indeterminate (and, as such, open to determination or yet to be determined). Consequently, the act of interpretation can involve a waiting for meaning or (if one chooses to emphasize the creativity of interpretation) a waiting *on* meaning, the service of meaning.

Waiting is not a purely passive exercise. Just as one can be bored doing many things, one can do many things as one waits. Waiting should not be prescribed as the only spiritual exercise of any value; instead, it should be understood as a special disposition that governs many such exercises. Even the most vigorously engaged political, social, or moral activity can be conceived as a mode of waiting, as a form of loving service ("waiting on"), even as it is a practice of indifference.

As a spiritual practice, waiting does not require the total absence in consciousness of all thoughts, feelings, and beliefs.[4] Rather, it is a discipline governed by the logic of indifference, a playful logic that does not mandate the elimination of all ideas but stipulates the refusal to be bound by them, fixed in place. That is why boredom is the great enemy of one who waits, why it thwarts the waiter. The bored person is cognitively and emotionally inert, as the Buddhists observed, like "a lump of butter too stiff for spreading." One can endure many trials in order to wait, and yet nevertheless be defeated by boredom.

Waiting is something that takes place *in time,* and boredom, of course, is a heightened awareness of the passing of time. In boredom, it is also true that the passing time is experienced as empty. One might choose to fill the emptiness with some determinate image, a specific goal: "I am waiting for this or that" or "at such and such a time, my waiting will be over." But this can also be the essence of diversion.

There is no religious need for waiting when the divine reality is hooked to some determinate image, when it is perceived as readily available to whomever is willing to pay the appropriate fees, confess the appropriate beliefs, invest in the proper kind of spiritual technology, and belong to the right religious community. Perhaps access to the sacred can even be provided by a television program, regularly shown at a particular time of the week or day. Here the risk is enormous that spirituality will itself become a diversion—from a certain religious point of view, the most dangerous diversion of all. If boredom is assuaged in the process, that point of view suggests, then it is better to be bored.

If waiting is a practice that may be especially vulnerable to boredom, it is nevertheless true that waiting (of the right kind) may be the best path to a cure for boredom (if what is really sought is a cure and not the mere suppression of symptoms). But waiting is no guarantee of a cure. That kind of control over the spiritual life, once again, is impossible. The achievement of a cure can never be "my" achievement, but will always have a gratuitous quality. If one could cure boredom, then one would never have to wait for a cure.

This is the most important thing that I can do about my boredom: I wait. But this waiting ought to be highly creative, attentive, detached. There can be no real love without this waiting—feelings of varying intensity, desires fulfilled or unfulfilled perhaps—but no love as enduring attention to the beloved, as constant readiness to be with and for the one loved.

NOTES

Introduction

1. Siegfried Wenzel has provided a survey and analysis of the medieval sources for the concept of acedia in his important work *The Sin of Sloth: Acedia in Medieval Thought and Literature* (Chapel Hill: University of North Carolina Press, 1976). I employ the term *acedia* in a somewhat less restricted sense than Wenzel does, not because I reject the criteria governing his usage, but because (as my discussion here indicates) I regard the straightforward application of those criteria to be frequently problematic.

William James's phenomenology of the "sick soul" comprises the sixth and seventh of his famous Gifford Lectures, published as *The Varieties of Religious Experience* (New York: Longmans, Green, 1902).

2. I use the word *semiotic* here in a very general sense to refer to any phenomenon involving signs and their interpretation. Later in my study, this term acquires a more precise and technical sense, as I explore some notions drawn from Peirce's semiotic theory and apply them to the analysis of boredom.

3. The "insights" to which I refer are those of the great American philosopher Charles S. Peirce. I have explored these insights most extensively in *Peirce's Philosophy of Religion* (Bloomington: Indiana University Press, 1989), while applying them directly to the topic of boredom in an essay on "Boredom

and the Religious Imagination," *Journal of the American Academy of Religion* 53 (1985): 75–91. (That essay serves as a prolegomenon to this book; some fragments of it, including the title, have been incorporated here.)

4. I observe that some of the basic features of this logic are similar, if not identical, to what Peirce described as the logic of abduction.

5. In my studies of Peirce, Edwards, and others, I have identified such a perspective as "theosemiotic," a word I felt to be ugly enough (like Peirce's "pragmaticism") to be safe from kidnappers.

Ignatius's exercises receive considerable attention in this book, but I only glance at Edwards's work on the affections. For a more extensive treatment of the latter, see my "Jonathan Edwards's Twelfth Sign," *International Philosophical Quarterly* 23 (1993): 153–62.

6. In addition to Wenzel's careful analysis of the medieval literature, such readers should consult Reinhard Kuhn's *Demon of Noontide: Ennui in Western Literature* (Princeton, N.J.: Princeton University Press, 1976). More recent, and somewhat more limited in scope, is Patricia Meyer Spacks's engaging study, *Boredom: A Literary History of a State of Mind* (Chicago: University of Chicago Press, 1995).

7. It is interesting to note that theologians consider the "demon of noontide" to be especially dangerous both at midday and during midlife, those times when individuals are regarded as being most vulnerable to boredom and distraction. Kuhn's study describes the dangers of the noon hour (*Demon of Noontide*, chap. 2). On the peculiar types of spiritual affliction characteristic of middle age, see Bernard Basset's *The Noonday Devil* (London: Sheed & Ward, 1978).

1. Portraying Acedia

1. Wenzel takes special pains to make this distinction. See his *Sin of Sloth*, especially 60–63. My interests here are philo-

sophical rather than strictly historical or linguistic, so that my concern is less with the technical usage of the term than with the sort of experience that it has been used to designate.

2. Aquinas, following Gregory, lists "idleness and laziness" among the "daughters" of acedia in his *Summa Theologica*, 2, part 2, question 35, article 4, "Reply to Objection 3."

3. Ibid., article 3.

4. The moral significance of boredom cannot be reduced to talk about the extent to which I am responsible for the quality of my own experiences. Such talk must extend to cases where someone might control the conditions that shape another person's experience; i.e., cases where I bore someone or am at least partially responsible for her boredom.

5. For a useful sketch of this background material (although one not limited to discourse about acedia), consult Morton Bloomfield's *Seven Deadly Sins* (East Lansing: Michigan State College Press, 1952), chap. 1, "The Pagan and Jewish Background."

6. Consider, as one example, Isaiah 42: 18ff., as well as the New Testament gloss on this text in Matthew 13: 9ff.

7. Arnold J. Band, ed., *Nahman of Bratslav: The Tales* (New York: Paulist Press, 1978), 34.

8. The writings of Abraham Heschel provide one example of such a perspective. See Heschel on the nature of *kavanah*, in *Man's Quest For God: Studies in Prayer and Symbolism* (New York: Charles Scribner's Sons, 1954), 11–14; and in *Between God and Man: An Interpretation of Judaism*, ed. Fritz A. Rothschild (New York: Free Press, 1959), 165–66.

9. Heschel, *Man's Quest for God*, 13.

10. Swami Prabhavananda and Christopher Isherwood, eds., *How to Know God: The Yoga Aphorisms of Patanjali* (New York: New American Library, 1969), part 1, aphorism 30, pp. 44–45.

11. In addition to the Prabhavananda-Isherwood interpretation of this sutra, examine the classical commentary of Vyasa,

supplemented with remarks by Swami Harharananda Aranya, in *Yoga Philosophy of Patanjali*, trans. P. N. Mukerji (Albany: State University of New York Press, 1983), 70–72.

12. See Edward Conze, *Buddhist Meditation* (London: George Allen & Unwin, 1956), 73–78; and C. A. F. Rhys Davids, ed., *A Buddhist Manual of Psychological Ethics* (Oriental Books Reprint, 1975), 310–15.

13. See Buddhagosa's *Visuddhimagga*, translated as *The Path of Purity* by Pe Maung Tin (London: Routledge & Kegan Paul, 1975), 550–51.

14. Davids, *Buddhist Manual*, 311.

15. "All things are full of weariness; a man cannot utter it; the eye is not satisfied with seeing, nor the ear filled with hearing. What has been is what will be, and what has been done is what will be done; and there is nothing new under the sun" (Ecclesiastes 1:8–9).

16. See Wenzel, *Sin of Sloth*, 5.

17. Wenzel comments on the Greek prehistory of the desert fathers' usage of this term; see ibid., 7.

18. T. S. Eliot, from his poem "Ash Wednesday," in the *Complete Poems and Plays: 1909–1950* (New York: Harcourt, Brace & World, 1971); see p. 61.

19. Louis Bouyer, *The Spirituality of the New Testament and the Fathers* (London: Burns & Oates, 1968), 384–87.

20. Wenzel, *Sin of Sloth*, 22.

21. I am in agreement with Kuhn when he argues that there is relatively little development in the concept of acedia in the period between the early reflections of Evagrius and Cassian and the medieval theology of Aquinas (Kuhn, *Demon of Noontide*, 55). In the interim, while there is considerable talk about acedia, practical talk about how it is best to be recognized, avoided, and remedied, there is no significant transformation in the manner in which it is portrayed or understood (although it does acquire a somewhat broader connotation; see note 29 below).

22. Aquinas, *Summa Theologica*, part II-II, question 35, article 1.

23. Ibid., article 3, "Reply to Objection 1." Compare, from a twentieth-century Thomist perspective, Josef Pieper's portrayal of acedia as a fundamental incapacity to enjoy leisure, and thus to affirm one's own being, in *Leisure: The Basis of Culture*, trans. Alexander Dru (New York: New American Library, 1963), 38–45.

24. Aquinas, *Summa Theologica*, part II-II, question 35, article 3, "Reply to Objection 3."

25. Ibid., article 4, "Reply to Objection 2."

26. Dante, *Purgatorio*, trans. John D. Sinclair (New York: Oxford University Press, 1975), 237. See also Sinclair's insightful commentary, 241–43.

27. Dante, *Inferno*, trans. John Sinclair (New York: Oxford University Press, 1972), 105.

28. Geoffrey Chaucer, *Complete Works*, ed. Walter K. Skeat (London: Oxford University Press, 1976), 699–702.

29. Wenzel's translation of *Fascilium Morum* (University Park: Pennsylvania State University Press, 1989), a fourteenth-century handbook for preachers, reveals that during this period acedia can still be understood as "boredom with respect to the good" (399). But the same text shows the extent to which, as Wenzel commented in his earlier study, this concept had "by 1300 grown so bulky." That comment appears in an extended analysis of the deterioration of the concept of acedia in chapter 7 of his *Sin of Sloth*, 164–87. (Once again, Wenzel refuses to conflate later talk about "spiritual dryness" or the "dark night of the soul" with the ancient and medieval discourse concerning acedia. My interest, however, is in exploring both the differences and the continuities among these phenomena, while treating them all as species of religious boredom.)

Alduous Huxley remarked on some of the same historical developments in his own very brief but thoughtful essay on "Accidie," in *On the Margin: Notes and Essays* (London: Chatto & Windus, 1923), 18–25.

30. Consult Robert Burton's classic work *The Anatomy of Melancholy*, ed. Floyd Dell and Paul Jordan-Smith (New York:

Farrar & Rinehart, 1927), especially the concluding section on "Religious Melancholy."

31. Ignatius of Loyola, *The Spiritual Exercises,* ed. Louis J. Puhl (Chicago: Loyola University Press, 1951), from the "Rules for Discernment of Spirits," no. 317.

32. Ibid., no. 322.

33. John of the Cross, *The Collected Works of St. John of the Cross,* trans. Kieran Kavanaugh and Otilio Rodriguez (Washington, D.C.: ICS Publications., 1979), from "The Dark Night," 310.

34. Ibid., 313.

35. James, *Varieties,* 127.

36. See James's essay on "The Moral Equivalent of War," in *Essays on Faith and Morals* (New York: World Publishing, 1962), 311–28.

37. James, *Varieties,* 131.

38. Ibid., 122.

39. Quoted from Baudelaire's poem "Destruction," in *The Flowers of Evil and Paris Spleen,* ed. William H. Crosby (Rochester: BOA Editions, 1991).

40. Samuel Beckett, *Waiting for Godot* (New York: Grove Press, 1954), 52.

41. Semiosis is the process consisting in the production and interpretation of signs. See my discussion in chapter 5.

42. For a sociological analysis of this second kind of boredom, resulting from the increased meaninglessness of information in a high-information society, see Orrin E. Klapp's *Overload and Boredom: Essays on the Quality of Life in the Information Society* (Westport, CT: Greenwood Press, 1986).

2. Killing Time

1. Henry David Thoreau, *Walden* (New York: W. W. Norton, 1951), 22. Thoreau describes (in the very next paragraph) persons who attempt to combat boredom by filling time with trivial amusements as being in "unconscious despair," leading lives of "quiet desperation."

NOTES

2. Blaise Pascal, *Pensées,* trans. A. J. Krailsheimer (Baltimore: Penguin Books, 1966), 36.

3. Ibid., 90.

4. Ibid., 159. (Peter H. Van Ness offers a consistently illuminating discussion of Pascal's assessment of the human "predicament" in the first chapter of his *Spirituality, Diversion, and Decadence: The Contemporary Predicament* [Albany: State University of New York Press, 1992].)

5. Pascal, *Pensées,* 66, 38.

6. Ibid., 148.

7. Ibid., 69.

8. Ibid., 75.

9. Ibid., 161.

10. Ibid., 43.

11. Søren Kierkegaard, *Either/Or,* trans. David F. Swenson and Lillian Marvin Swenson (Princeton, N.J.: Princeton University Press, 1959), 1:281.

12. Ibid., 282.

13. While the judgment of any artwork as "boring" is most typically interpreted as a negative evaluation, it would be a mistake to transform such an interpretation into a general axiological principle. Some artists (Andy Warhol, Samuel Beckett, John Cage) appeared not to regard bored responses to their work as something that must be avoided at all cost. Where an artwork is designed to edify or transform rather than simply amuse those who contemplate it, boredom cannot be altogether ruled out of the responses foreseen or intended by the artist.

For a discussion of the important role that elements of boredom and redundancy can play in the aesthetic experience, see Dick Higgins's essay on "Boredom and Danger," in *Breaking the Sound Barrier,* ed. G. Battcock (New York: Dutton, 1981), 20–27.

14. Kierkegaard, *Either/Or,* 1:36.

15. Ibid., 1:287.

16. This "poetizing" of existence is most carefully described in Kierkegaard's *Concluding Unscientific Postscript,* trans. David Swenson and Walter Lowrie (Princeton, N.J.: Princeton Univer-

sity Press, 1941), 347ff.; but it is most brilliantly portrayed in *Either/Or*, especially in "The Diary of a Seducer."

17. Kierkegaard, *Either/Or*, 1:289.

18. Ibid., 1:220.

19. Kierkegaard, *The Sickness unto Death*, trans. Alastair Hannay, (New York: Penguin Books, 1989), 44–45.

20. In a passage that echoes his satirical critique of the builders of the Tower of Babel, Kierkegaard compares such an individual to one who distracts himself with the construction of a "huge building" that *he himself* does not occupy. See *Sickness unto Death*, 74. (Gabriel Marcel's philosophical meditation on this phenomenon of spiritual "uneasiness," as it is portrayed by Kierkegaard, Pascal, and others, merits attention. Consult *Problematic Man* [New York: Herder & Herder, 1967]).

21. Kierkegaard, *Sickness unto Death*, 73.

22. Martin Heidegger, *The Fundamental Concepts of Metaphysics*, trans. William McNeill and Nicholas Walker (Bloomington: Indiana University Press, 1995), 77–79.

For a brilliant theological appropriation and extension of Heidegger's insights about boredom, consider Jean-Luc Marion's *God without Being*, trans. Thomas A. Carlson (Chicago: University of Chicago Press, 1991), especially 115–38.

23. Heidegger, *Fundamental Concepts*, 283. Heidegger's identification of boredom as a "way of being" does not necessarily conflict with my earlier description of boredom, following Pascal, as a kind of "feeling." Rather, Heidegger's analysis makes it clear that here our primary concern is not with any mere flash of feeling or momentary experience, but with powerful habits of feeling—habits that can dramatically shape the way we perceive the world around us (even as they represent responses and adaptations to that world).

24. Ibid., 90.

25. Ibid., 101.

26. Ibid., 97.

27. Ibid., 100.

28. Ibid., 92.

29. Ibid., 118–19.

30. Ibid., 135.

31. Ibid., 138.

32. Ibid., 145.

33. Ibid., 135.

34. Martin Heiddegger, "What is Metaphysics?," trans. R. F. C. Hull and Alan Crick, in *Existence and Being* (London: Vision Press, 1949), 364.

35. Heidegger, *Fundamental Concepts,* 275.

36. Ibid., 283.

37. Ibid., 351. The religious features of Heidegger's philosophy are both identified and carefully circumscribed by John Caputo in his study of *The Mystical Element in Heidegger's Thought* (New York: Fordham University Press, 1986). I pursue the same analogy that Caputo exposes between Heidegger and the mystics, with some brief comments, in chapter 3.

38. Wittgenstein supplies a parallel to my observation about the ambiguity of "awakening" with his own puzzling over the difficulty experienced in deciding whether to label the verb "to sleep" as either active or passive. (I owe the insight from Wittgenstein to my colleague Gordon Bearn, author of *Waking to Wonder: Wittgenstein's Existential Investigations* [Albany: State University of New York Press, 1996].)

39. Heidegger, *Fundamental Concepts,* 195, 266–73.

40. Consider Paul Tillich's theological investigation of this type of courage as a response to the anxiety induced by the awareness of death, by the threat of nonbeing, by the experience of emptiness and meaninglessness, in *The Courage to Be* (New Haven, Conn.: Yale University Press, 1952).

41. Aquinas, *Summa Theologica,* part II-II, question 136, article 3, "Reply to Objections."

42. Ignatius of Loyola, *Spiritual Exercises,* no. 13; see also nos. 318–21 in "Rules for Discernment of Spirits."

43. Francis de Sales, *Introduction to the Devout Life* (New York: Doubleday, 1972), 254; see also 92–93 for advice about coping with the problem of spiritual dryness.

44. Arthur Green and Barry W. Holtz, ed. and trans., *Your Word Is Fire: The Hasidic Masters on Contemplative Prayer* (New York: Schocken Books, 1977), 90, 93. See, also, the comments on distraction in the editors' introduction, 14–15.

45. Ibid., 94–95.

46. Ibid., 30.

47. Shunryu Suzuki, *Zen Mind, Beginner's Mind*, ed. Trudy Dixon (New York: Weatherhill, 1970), 34.

48. Thich Nhat Hanh, *The Miracle of Mindfulness: A Manual on Meditation*, trans. Mobi Ho (Boston: Beacon Press, 1975), 40.

49. Thich Nhat Hanh employs the metaphor of a bridge; Suzuki uses that of a "swinging door." See Thich Nhat Hanh, *Miracle of Mindfulness*, 15, and Suzuki, *Zen Mind*, 29.

50. Green and Holtz, *Your Word Is Fire*, 48, 63.

51. Ignatius of Loyola, *Spiritual Exercises*, no. 258.

52. Suzuki, *Zen Mind*, 109; see also 110–20.

3. Nothing Matters

1. Among the many places that James makes this argument, consider the collection of essays in *The Will to Believe* (New York: Dover, 1956), especially the title essay and "Is Life Worth Living?"—the first two essays in the book.

2. Ignatius of Loyola, *Spiritual Exercises*, no. 23.

3. Ibid., no. 179.

4. Karl Rahner, "The Ignatian Mysticism of Joy in the World," in *Theological Investigations* (New York: Seabury Press, 1974), 3:291.

5. Karl Rahner, "The Logic of Concrete Individual Knowledge in Ignatius Loyola," in *The Dynamic Element in the Church*, trans. W. J. O'Hara (New York: Herder & Herder, 1967), 155.

6. Ibid., 169.

7. Ignatius of Loyola, *Spiritual Exercises*, no. 330.

8. John of the Cross, "Dark Night," 321.

9. Ibid., 323.

10. Ibid., 331.

11. Francis de Sales, *Treatise on the Love of God,* trans. John K. Ryan (New York: Doubleday, 1963), 2:105ff.

12. Ibid., 119.

13. Ibid., 120.

14. Ibid., 127.

15. Ibid., 136.

16. Consult the Prabhavananda-Isherwood edition of the Yoga Sutras (*How to Know God,* 21–22; commentary on sutras 15 and 16 of book 1) concerning nonattachment as the opposite of common boredom or a cold indifference.

17. *The Bhagavadgita,* trans. Kees Bolle (Berkeley: University of California Press, 1979), 2:39–72, 29–37.

18. Meister Eckhart, "About Disinterest," in *Meister Eckhart: A Modern Translation,* trans. Raymond Blakney (San Francisco: Harper & Row, 1941), 85.

19. Ibid., 88.

20. Green and Holtz, *Your Word Is Fire,* 56.

21. Ibid., 58.

22. Takuan Soho, *The Unfettered Mind,* trans. William Scott Wilson (Tokyo: Kodansha International, 1986), 33.

23. *The Way of Life According to Lao Tzu,* trans. Witter Bynner (New York: Capricorn Books, 1944), 72.

24. T. P. Kasulis offers a fine critical discussion of both the similarities and the differences between Zen and Heideggerian perspectives on "No-Mind" in his *Zen Action, Zen Person* (Honolulu: University of Hawaii Press, 1981), especially chap. 4.

25. Immanuel Kant, *Critique of Judgment,* trans. Werner S. Pluhar (Indianapolis: Hackett Publishing, 1987), 92.

26. Ibid., bk. 1, no. 9.

27. Ibid., bk. 1, no. 22, "General Remark."

28. Ibid., bk. 2, no. 59.

29. Friedrich Schiller, *On the Aesthetic Education of Man,* ed. and trans. Elizabeth M. Wilkinson and L. A. Willoughby (Oxford: Clarendon Press, 1982), letter 22, 153.

30. Ibid., letter 21, 147.

31. On the relationship between contemplation and play, consult Pieper's *Leisure: The Basis of Culture*, especially 32; also Hugo Rahner's *Man at Play* (New York: Herder & Herder, 1967).

32. Schiller, *Aesthetic Education*, letter 21, 145.

33. Ibid., letter 14, 97.

34. For a contrasting account of the nature of aesthetic judgment, refer to Barbara Herrnstein Smith's *Contingencies of Value* (Cambridge, Mass.: Harvard University Press, 1988), especially the critical remarks about Kant in chap. 4.

Note that Smith, like both Kant and Schiller, incorporates a notion of "cognitive play" in her description of our typical response to works of art. This "playing with" beliefs and interests, rather than simply suppressing all beliefs and interests, best captures the sense of the word *disinterestedness* as I am using it in this discussion. See Smith's earlier work, *On the Margins of Discourse: The Relations of Literature to Language* (Chicago: University of Chicago Press, 1978).

35. C. S. Peirce, *Semiotic and Significs: The Correspondence between Charles S. Peirce and Victoria Lady Welby*, ed. Charles S. Hardwick (Bloomington: Indiana University Press, 1977), 77, letter of 23 December 1908.

36. This description of Musement appears in Peirce's essay "A Neglected Argument for the Reality of God." Consult the edition of Peirce's *Collected Papers*, ed. Charles Hartshorne, Paul Weiss, and Arthur Burks (Cambridge, Mass.: Harvard University Press, 1935, 1958), vol. 6: paras. 458–61. (I refer in this study to the Harvard edition of Peirce's *Collected Papers* rather than Indiana University Press's more recent, chronological, edition, *Writings of Charles S. Peirce*, because I draw so heavily upon some of Peirce's later essays, yet to be published in the Indiana edition.) I provided a brief comparison of Peirce and Schiller on this topic in *Peirce's Philosophy of Religion*, 128–29.

37. Schiller, *Aesthetic Education*, letter 23, 165.

38. Peirce's early theory of abduction drew upon his extended meditations on the syllogism, distinguishing but relating the various modes of inference as all being reducible to Barbara. (See,

for example, the material in *Collected Papers*, 2:461–516 and 2:619–44.) By 1908, the year that his "Neglected Argument" was published, Peirce had come to perceive abduction, deduction, and induction as three distinctive but nevertheless interdependent "stages of inquiry." It is this later theory of abduction that will contribute most to the understanding of boredom as a semiotic phenomenon (in chapter 5 below).

39. Schiller, *Aesthetic Education*, letter 12, 81.

40. Peirce, *Collected Papers*, 5:181ff.

41. Ibid., 2:623.

42. For example, the belief that "loving persons display generosity to those whom they love" suggests but does not necessarily entail the conclusion (when I observe someone's generous behavior) that a given person is loving. The person may be disingenuous, acting out of self-interest, and so forth.

43. Peirce, *Collected Papers*, 6:461.

44. Martin Heidegger, *Discourse on Thinking*, trans. John M. Anderson and E. Hans Freund (New York: Harper & Row, 1966), 61.

45. Ibid., 54ff., 67ff.

46. Karl Rahner, "Logic of Concrete Individual Knowledge," 161.

47. I have argued that Peirce himself understood Musement as a kind of experimental process; see *Peirce's Philosophy of Religion*, 134, 139.

48. Paul's letter to the Philippians, 4:11–13.

4. Ritual, Redundancy, and the Religious Imagination

1. Mihalyi Csikszentmihalyi, *Beyond Boredom and Anxiety* (San Francisco: Jossey-Bass, 1977).

2. Abraham Maslow, *Religions, Values and Peak-Experiences* (Baltimore: Penguin Books, 1976).

3. Samuel Beckett, *Proust* (New York: Grove Press, 1931), 7ff. For Beckett (and for Proust) habit, as second nature, "keeps us in

ignorance of the first." As such, habit and boredom are symptoms of a certain existential "forgetfulness," a terrible, even if comfortable, diminution of awareness.

4. For remarks on boredom as a plague of modern education, see Sean Healy's *Boredom, Self and Culture* (London: Associated University Presses, 1984), especially the concluding chapter on "Boredom and the School."

5. My question and subsequent analysis should not be taken as an indication that I suppose redundancy to be the only factor contributing to the boredom that can infect religious ritual behavior. These rituals do not occur in a vacuum, but are enacted by the members of specific religious communities, with their own complex histories and theologies. For contemporary practitioners, a lack of connectedness with those historical traditions and a confusion or disagreement about doctrinal issues are two additional factors that might mitigate the effectiveness of ritual.

6. This dictum is borrowed from Gregory Bateson's important essay on "Redundancy and Coding" in *Steps to an Ecology of Mind* (New York: Ballantine Books, 1980), see 422.

7. I am especially indebted to the "broader conception of noise" employed by Orrin E. Klapp in his work, *Opening and Closing: Strategies of Information Adaptation in Society* (Cambridge: Cambridge University Press, 1978).

8. See Klapp's *Overload and Boredom*, 70.

9. It seems reasonable to hypothesize that the sort of boredom that can afflict older persons is often a consequence of the information underload that results from diminished hearing capacity. Unable to process information from a conversation or a television program or a public speech as anything other than noise, one might be tempted simply to "tune it out." (I am reminded of an elderly relation of mine who habitually turns down the volume on his hearing aid so as not to endure what he experiences all too frequently as the painful "noise" in a restaurant, on a streetcorner, or even in his own living room.)

10. For an acute analysis of the importance of habits in shap-

ing our response to music, consult Leonard B. Meyer's "Meaning in Music and Information Theory" in *Music, the Arts, and Ideas* (Chicago: University of Chicago Press, 1967), 5–21. Meyer suggests that while habits help to generate meaning in musical experience, those musical stimuli to which one responds habitually are themselves neither meaningful nor meaningless, but rather "neutral with respect to meaning" (see 9). Something must disturb our unthinking, habitual responses in order for such stimuli to be lifted into the realm of awareness and become meaningful. Meyer's essay is loaded with insight. Following Peirce, however, I conceive of meaning in more broadly semiotic terms as being embodied, potentially, in habits of feeling, thought, and conduct. Our habit responses to various signs, various stimuli, constitute an interpretation of their meaning for us, even when we are not able to formulate that meaning in explicit conceptual terms, indeed, even when we are not fully *aware* of it!

11. Compare Marx's concerns about religion-as-anaesthetic with Samuel Beckett's suspicion of habit's "dulling" effects, already noted above.

12. Pascal, *Pensées*, 152.

13. Ibid., 274.

14. See Peirce's famous essay on "The Fixation of Belief" in his *Collected Papers*, especially 5:370ff.

15. Oddly enough, this is true (as I have already tried to suggest) even for beliefs of the sort "*X* is not interesting," a fact that helps to explain how I can be bored without being fully aware of my condition or without admitting it, while others might be able to infer that this is the case by observing my behavior.

16. As samples of Peirce's numerous remarks on self-control, refer to the *Collected Papers*, 5:418ff., 5:553ff.

17. Peter Van Ness's *Spirituality, Diversion, and Decadence* describes, in a compelling manner, contemporary spiritual disciplines *both* as methods of habit formation (especially "brief" habits that signal self-mastery) *and* as modes of resisting unde-

sirable habituation (of the sort that advertisers or oppressive governments might seek to inculcate in individuals in order to control their behavior). See, especially, chap. 2.

18. Ludwig Wittgenstein, *Zettel,* eds. G. E. M. Anscombe and von Wright, (Berkeley: University of California Press, 1967), no. 642.

19. My perspective is Peircean, but arguments that the imagination plays a constructive role in sense perception have been commonplace in post-Kantian philosophy. Consult Mary Warnock's careful review of some of these arguments in *Imagination* (Berkeley: University of California Press, 1976). It is important to note that Wittgenstein is among the philosophers that she considers (part 4, especially 190ff.). Despite his suspicion of any simple analogy between mental images and sense impressions, Wittgenstein's meditations on "aspect seeing" underscore the interpretive element in perception.

20. Peirce, *Collected Papers,* 5:115–19, 5:151–57, 5:181ff.

21. Wittgenstein, *Zettel,* no. 642.

22. Warnock agrees that the distinction is a problematic one (see *Imagination,* 193).

23. As my remarks about this example will indicate, I adhere to the perspective that perceptual judgments, always abductive in form, can involve the application of certain emotions, as well as conceptions, to some object.

24. Thich Nhat Hanh, *Miracle of Mindfulness,* 50–51, 91–92, 116–18.

25. For example, Peirce, *Collected Papers,* 5:480–81, 5:517, 6:286.

26. Even Kierkegaard, despite his worries about the imagination, understood its transformative power, its truly ethical and religious significance. A number of studies note this ambivalence in Kierkegaard toward the imagination; one of the most insightful is M. Jamie Ferreira's *Transforming Vision: Imagination and Will in Kierkegaardian Faith* (Oxford: Oxford University Press, 1991).

27. Bateson, *Steps to an Ecology of Mind,* 135, in the essay "Style, Grace, and Information in Primitive Art."

28. Augustin M. de la Pena, *The Psychobiology of Cancer: Automatization and Boredom in Health and Disease* (New York: Praeger, 1983), 36. (Peirce's "law of mind" also stipulates that as ideas gain in generality they lose something of their intensity, an insight that I develop in my semiotic of boredom.)

29. Warnock, *Imagination,* 202–3.

30. Mary Warnock, "Religious Imagination," in *Religious Imagination,* ed. James P. Mackey (Edinburgh: Edinburgh University Press, 1986), 147.

31. For a brilliant psychological defense of the importance of boredom, especially in the experience of children, refer to Adam Phillip's essay "On Being Bored" in *On Kissing, Tickling and Being Bored* (Cambridge, Mass.: Harvard University Press, 1993), 68–78. From a very different perspective, but in a similar vein, see Joseph Brodsky's "In Praise of Boredom," in *On Grief and Reason: Essays* (New York: Farrar, Straus & Giroux, 1995), 104–13.

5. Boredom, Semiosis, and Spiritual Exercises

1. The proposition that every thought is a sign and the corresponding theory that all human experience can be conceived as semiosis were articulated by Peirce early in his philosophical career, most notably in two 1868 essays published in the *Journal of Speculative Philosophy,* entitled "Questions Concerning Certain Faculties Claimed for Man" and "Some Consequences of Four Incapacities." See in the *Collected Papers,* 5:213–317.

2. It is equally the case that what is boring to one person at a given point in time may later prove to be of interest to that same person. Individuals develop interests in all sorts of ways and for a great variety of reasons. A flashlight on the kitchen counter may seem the perfect candidate for an "intrinsically boring" household object. But a power failure during an evening storm may suddenly enhance its significance.

This is a rather mundane example of how one might "develop interest" in a thing. The example is inspired by Walker Percy's much more imaginative and compelling explorations (numerous, both in his fiction and his essays) of how sudden danger or disaster can dramatically transform our ordinary perceptions of things, stimulate a new and deeper insight into their significance. See, for one example, his thought-experiment with boredom, in *Lost in the Cosmos: The Last Self-Help Book* (New York: Simon & Schuster, 1984), 73–75.

3. From this perspective, while both persons might "appear" to understand the conversation equally well (they both know the language and have a clear comprehension of the subject matter), it may be possible to describe one person as having a greater "depth" of understanding than the other. Symbols are multivalent, and while not perfectly indeterminate in meaning, nevertheless infinitely rich in potential meanings. One person might have access to certain meanings, kinds, or levels of information that the other lacks.

4. The analysis here is Peircean. What I do in response to my boredom can be regarded as an "interpretant" of that boredom conceived as a sign. As Peirce made clear in a later commentary on his own "pragmatic maxim," the most fully meaningful interpretant will consist not in some discrete action, but in a pattern or habit of action. Further, meaning is not isolated or embodied in the actions of a single individual, so that what other persons might do in response to my boredom is also an interpretation of what that experience means. See Peirce's *Collected Papers,* 5:402, especially notes 2 and 3.

5. Percy, *Lost in the Cosmos,* 23–29.

6. See Peirce's *Collected Papers,* 2:641–44. A simple example of such an abductive hypothesis would be the suggestion that "this dog must be a Wheaten terrier." For an example of the corresponding habit of thought that might have helped to yield such a conclusion in any particular case, consider the inductively established claim that "all Wheaten terriers have a soft, silky coat of almost human-like hair."

7. I explored Peirce's essentialism in "Habits and Essences," *Transactions of the Charles S. Peirce Society* 20 (1984): 147–67.

8. Sample the collection of material in *A Hopkins Reader*, ed. John Pick, (New York: Doubleday, 1966), 85–124.

9. Peirce, *Collected Papers*, 5:119.

10. The phrase is borrowed from Arthur C. Danto's work in aesthetics bearing this title. *The Transfiguration of the Commonplace*, (Cambridge, Mass.: Harvard University Press, 1981).

11. Peirce, *Collected Papers*, 6:104.

12. Ibid., 6:149.

13. Ibid., 6:145.

14. Ibid., 5:291.

15. Ibid., 5:292.

16. Pascal, *Pensées*, 67.

17. This is a standard definition of the term. See, for example, the first definition of "exercise" in *Webster's New Collegiate Dictionary* (1981), 397, as "the act of bringing into play or realizing in action."

18. Peirce, *Collected Papers*, 6:458 (from Peirce's 1908 essay "A Neglected Argument for the Reality of God").

Practice makes perfect. But having recommended engaging in this exercise for such a small percentage of one's conscious time, as something to be "pursued in odd half hours," perhaps Peirce had some concern that if Musement were to be greatly prolonged it might cease to be "refreshing" and become . . . boring.

19. Ibid., 6:493.

20. These essays appeared in the *Journal of Speculative Philosophy* in 1868. See, especially, "Some Consequences of Four Incapacities," 5:295ff.

It is interesting to note that Peirce shared Wittgenstein's suspicion of traditional philosophical talk (e.g., in Hume) about "mental images"; see 5:300ff.

21. Peirce, *Collected Papers*, 5:296–97.

22. Ibid., 5:308.

23. I mean "more or less" depending on the interpreter's quality of attention, the extent to which it is either disinterested or molded by powerful habits of expectation. See my remarks below.

24. Peirce, *Collected Papers*, 5:297.

The "Neglected Argument" makes it clear that Peirce considered a vague belief in God to be instinctive in human beings. I explored his thinking about this issue in *Peirce's Philosophy of Religion*, especially 96–101 and 130–32.

25. The definition of meditation as a practice of attention is misleadingly simple. I have investigated some of the complexities generated by such a definition in the essay "Poinsot on the Semiotics of Awareness," *American Catholic Philosophical Quarterly*, 68 (1994): 395–408.

26. Writings in Buddhist Abhidharma texts, for example, go into considerable detail about different kinds of attention.

27. Peirce, *Collected Papers*, 6:437.

28. Ignatius of Loyola, *Spiritual Exercises*, no. 1.

29. Peirce, *Collected Papers*, 6:467.

30. For a clear discussion of this Ignatian strategy, consult Alexander Brou, S.J., *Ignatian Methods of Prayer*, trans. William Young, S.J. (Milwaukee: Bruce Publishing, 1949), 146–67.

31. These insights are articulated in Edwards's remarkable work *A Treatise Concerning Religious Affections*, ed. John E. Smith (New Haven, Conn.: Yale University Press, 1959).

William Spohn provides a lucid and sensitive comparison of Ignatius and Edwards on the topic of discernment in his essay "Finding God in All Things: Jonathan Edwards and Ignatius Loyola," in *Finding God in All Things: Essays in Honor of Michael J. Buckley*, ed. Michael J. Himes and Stephen J. Pope (New York: Crossroad, 1996), 244–61.

32. Consider again the important commentary appended as later footnotes to Peirce's essay on "How To Make Our Ideas Clear." *Collected Papers*, 5:402, especially note 2.

33. Jonathan Edwards, *The Distinguishing Marks of a Work of the Spirit of God*, in *The Works of Jonathan Edwards*, ed. C. Goen (New Haven, Conn.: Yale University Press, 1972), 4:238.

34. Edwards, *Religious Affections*, 452.

35. Ibid., 434.

Postlude

1. The etymology of *wait* is instructive for the purposes of this discussion. It derives from the verb *to watch* and is associated with *wake*. (I owe this insight to Dennis Marshall.)

2. Hermann Hesse, *Siddhartha* (New York: Bantam Books, 1982).

3. From the Gospel of Mark, 13:33.

4. The total emptying of consciousness may be a goal of certain religious traditions, but this goal is easily caricatured and misunderstood, as I think it is by Arthur Danto in his essay on "*Brahma*, Boredom and Release," the third chapter of *Mysticism and Morality* (New York: Columbia University Press, 1987), 46–64.

INDEX

abduction, 96–102, 151–52, 186;
and induction, 144–48, 158–59;
and the imagination, 125–29
acedia, 2, 4, 11–40, 43, 58, 63–64,
79, 80, 114, 143, 178, 179
aesthetics, 7, 50–52, 147, 181; and
disinterestedness, 86–94
apatheia, 22, 35–36
Aquinas, Saint Thomas, 6, 12, 13,
23–25, 32, 64–65, 142
attention, 15, 16, 37, 61–64, 73,
116–17, 143, 153–54, 156–60
attunement: boredom as
fundamental, 54–60. *See also*
Heidegger, Martin
awakening (being awake), 59–60,
99, 157–58, 183

Baudelaire, Charles, 33
Beckett, Samuel, 33, 106, 111
Buddhism, 128–29; boredom in,
18–19, 36, 48; on distraction in
meditation, 67–70; on emptiness, 19, 48, 84–85

Cassian, John, 23, 24, 39, 64
Chaucer, Geoffrey, 27

Christianity: boredom in, 19–31
consolation: as spiritual joy, 23,
28–29, 76–78
Csikszentmihalyi, Mihalyi, 105

Dante Alighieri, 6, 26
dark night of the soul, 2, 6, 11,
29–31, 79–80. *See also* John of
the Cross, Saint
death, 33–34, 41, 45, 60, 61, 102–3
demon of noontide, 10, 20, 176
desolation, 11, 27–29, 65, 76–79.
See also dryness, spiritual;
Ignatius of Loyola, Saint
despair, 25, 27, 32, 34, 42, 53–54
detachment, 7, 36, 83, 102, 129,
159, 161
discernment, 35–36, 74–78, 111,
130
disinterestedness, 7, 19, 82–104,
159, 186. *See also* detachment;
indifference
distraction, 7, 18, 24, 62–71, 149
diversion, 7, 41–60; as forgetfulness, 52, 56, 59
drowsiness: as "daughter" of
acedia, 2, 16, 115

197

"dryness," spiritual, 11, 13, 24, 30, 143
Duns Scotus, John, 146

Eckhart, Meister, 83
Edwards, Jonathan, 9, 163–65
Eliot, T. S., 22
emptiness, 51, 55, 57, 60, 118, 135, 137
ennui, 12, 34–35
Evagrius, 20–22, 24

fortitude, 64–65
Francis de Sales, Saint, 65, 80–82

habit, 8, 37, 105–32, 147–48; and beliefs, 120–21, 126–31, 144–48; and imagination, 124–32; as skill, 131–33, 148, 151, 158–59; and volition, 122–28
Heidegger, Martin, 7, 54–60, 100–101, 142
Hinduism: boredom in, 18
Hopkins, Gerard Manley, 146

Ignatius of Loyola, Saint, 9, 27–29, 65, 67, 161–63; on discernment, 74–79; on the imagination, 130
imagination, 3, 15, 31, 38, 40, 124–35; in Kant, 87–89
indeterminacy, 56, 83, 91, 98–99, 102, 126–27
indifference, 36, 57, 69, 75–83; as a state of readiness, 75, 78, 119, 145. See also logic of indifference
information: and boredom, 2, 8, 110–35, 139–40, 148. See also redundancy
interpretation, 3, 4, 38, 119, 137, 139, 171; as abduction, 146–50; emotions (feelings) as, 3, 45, 99–100, 128, 140, 152–53, 162–63

James, William, 2, 6, 31–33, 73
Jesus Christ, 1, 20, 169, 170
John of the Cross, Saint, 6, 29–31, 33, 79–80, 143
Judaism: boredom in, 16–18; on distraction in prayer, 66–67; on indifference, 83–84

Kant, Immanuel, 87–89
Kierkegaard, Søren, 7, 25, 49–54, 93–94, 147

logic of indifference, 9, 72–104. See also abduction; indifference
love: and boredom, 13, 26, 34, 37–38, 58, 64–65, 150; as caritas, 13, 22, 64–65, 81, 103
"lukewarmness," 26, 30, 31

Maslow, Abraham, 105–6
meaning, 5, 8, 15, 32–33, 34, 40, 61, 63, 112, 128, 139, 148, 189
meditation, 20, 30, 31, 37, 102, 134, 153–63
melancholy: Renaissance conception of, 27, 31, 153
mindfulness, 43; and breathing, 69–71
Musement, 95–102, 129–30, 144–46, 163–64; as the logic of abduction, 96–102

noise: in information theory, 111, 114, 118
nothing (nothingness), 33–34, 42, 44, 51, 60, 82, 84, 90, 137, 144

Pascal, Blaise: on diversion, 7, 44–48, 142; on habit, 120–21

Paul, Saint, 60, 61, 65, 85, 103–4
Peirce, Charles S., 3, 9, 95–102,
   106, 144–53; on habit, 120–21.
   See also Musement; semiotic(s)
play, 127, 133–34; in Kant's
   aesthetics, 87–89; in Peirce's
   philosophy, 95–110, 129–30,
   145–50; in Schiller's aesthetics,
   89–95. *See also* Musement
poverty of spirit, 60, 85
prayer, 17–18, 20, 30, 66–67, 160

Rahner, Karl: on the logic of
   indifference, 75–78, 101–2, 161
redundancy, 8, 107–32, 147. *See
   also* habit; information
ritual, 117–18, 123, 188

self-control, 22, 36, 38, 73–74;
   and attention, 119–21
semiotic, 2, 8, 15, 21, 30, 80, 133,
   175; of boredom, 36, 80, 86,
   100, 136–66, 192; breakdown,
   3–4, 31, 113–16, 125, 137–42,
   148; and meaning, 63, 148; and
   semiosis, 5, 36, 143, 162, 180.

See also Peirce, Charles S.
Schiller, Friedrich, 89–96; on the
   Spieltrieb, 89–93. *See also*
   Musement
sloth, 12, 19, 23, 27
spiritual combat: against
   boredom, 20–21, 29, 32, 38, 64,
   65, 69, 85
spiritual exercise, 12, 20, 25, 27–
   29, 30, 79, 128, 154–65, 162;
   Musement as, 156–61; waiting
   as, 171–72. *See also* Ignatius of
   Loyola, Saint; meditation;
   prayer

Taoism, 85, 91
Thich Nhat Hanh, 68–69
Thoreau, Henry David, 41
time, 39–40, 41–42, 44, 55–56,
   107

waiting, 9, 59, 70, 83, 167–73
Weil, Simone, 167
Wittgenstein, Ludwig, 124, 126
work: as proposed remedy for
   boredom, 23, 51, 53

STUDIES IN RELIGION AND CULTURE

Edmund N. Santurri
Perplexity in the Moral Life: Philosophical and Theological Considerations

Robert P. Scharlemann
Inscriptions and Reflections: Essays in Philosophical Theology

James DiCenso
Hermeneutics and the Disclosure of Truth: A Study in the Work of Heidegger, Gadamer, and Ricoeur

David Lawton
Faith, Text, and History: The Bible in English

Robert P. Scharlemann, editor
Theology at the End of the Century: A Dialogue on the Postmodern

Robert P. Scharlemann, editor
Negation and Theology

Lynda Sexson
Ordinarily Sacred

David E. Klemm and William Schweiker, editors
Meanings in Texts and Actions: Questioning Paul Ricoeur

Guyton B. Hammond
Conscience and Its Recovery: From the Frankfurt School to Feminism

Roger Poole
Kierkegaard: The Indirect Communication

John D. Barbour
Versions of Deconversion: Autobiography and the Loss of Faith

Gary L. Ebersole
Captured by Texts: Puritan to Postmodern Images of Indian Captivity

David Chidester
Savage Systems: Colonialism and Comparative Religion in Southern Africa

Laurie L. Patton and Wendy Doniger, editors
Myth and Method

Orrin F. Summerell, editor
The Otherness of God

Langdon Gilkey
Creationism on Trial: Evolution and God at Little Rock

Michael L. Raposa
Boredom and the Religious Imagination